On Lower Lakeland Fells

Also by Bob Allen   On High Lakeland Fells

View to the Helm Crag ridge and Helvellyn, from Holme Fell

ON LOWER LAKELAND FELLS

The 50 Best Walks

Bob Allen

MICHAEL JOSEPH
London

MICHAEL JOSEPH LTD

Published by the Penguin Group
27 Wrights Lane, London W8 5TZ, England
Viking Penguin Inc., 40 West 23rd Street, New York, New York 10010, USA
Penguin Books Australia Ltd, Ringwood, Victoria, Australia
Penguin Books Canada Ltd, 2801 John Street, Markham, Ontario,
Canada L3R 1B4
Penguin Books (NZ) Ltd, 182–190 Wairau Road, Auckland 10, New Zealand

Penguin Books Ltd, Registered Offices: Harmondsworth, Middlesex, England

First published 1990

Typeset in 11 on 12pt Linotron Goudy Old Style by
Goodfellow and Egan Ltd, Cambridge

Colour reproduction by Anglia Graphics, Bedford

Printed and bound in Great Britain by Butler and Tanner, Frome, Somerset

A CIP catalogue record for this book is available from the British Library

ISBN 0 7181 3369 2

CONTENTS

Introduction   7

Walks in the North-West

 1. High Rigg   13
 2. Nab Crags (Thirlmere)   17
 3. Latrigg   21
 4. Catbells and Derwentwater   25
 5. High Doat and Castle Crag   29
 6. Jopplety How and Brund Fell   33
 7. Great Crag (Borrowdale)   37
 8. Barrow and Outerside   41
 9. Sale Fell   45
10. Mellbreak   49
11. Carling Knott and Holme Wood   53
12. Rannerdale Knotts   57
13. Green Crag and Haystacks   61
14. Fleetwith Pike   65
15. Circuit of Buttermere   69

Walks in the North-East

16. Bowscale Fell and Bannerdale Crags   75
17. Artle Crag and Gatescarth   79
18. Place Fell   83
19. Ullswater Lakeshore   87
20. Beda Fell and The Nab   91
21. Sheffield Pike   95
22. Satura Crag and Angletarn Pikes   99
23. Gowbarrow Fell   103
24. Hallin Fell   107
25. Gill Crag Ridge and Dovedale   111
26. Gray Crag   115

Walks in the South-West

27. Black Combe   121
28. Muncaster Fell   125
29. Buckbarrow   129
30. Latterbarrow and Whin Rigg   133
31. Wallowbarrow   137
32. Border End and Hard Knott   141
33. High Gait Crags   145
34. Harter Fell   149
35. Green Crag and Stanley Force   153
36. Red How and Cold Pike   157
37. Yewdale Fells   161
38. Lingmoor Fell   165
39. Blake Rigg   169
40. Tarn Crag (Easedale)   173
41. Blea Rigg and Great Castle How   177
42. Whitbarrow Scar   181
43. Holme Fell   185

Walks in the South-East

44. Elter Water, Colwith and Little Langdale   191
45. Loughrigg Fell   195
46. Grasmere and Rydal   199
47. Butter Crag and Allcock Tarn   203
48. Wansfell Pike and Troutbeck   207
49. Silver How   211
50. Helm Crag and the Easedale Ridge   215

Acknowledgements   219

Index   221

INTRODUCTION

This book is an illustrated collection of fifty of the very best shorter fellwalks in the Lake District (though I have deliberately included half a dozen of the best 'valley-bottom' walks as well). Even while I was completing *On High Lakeland Fells* I was aware that all the emphasis in that book was on the 'High', that I was missing out some marvellous fells whose only difference was their comparative lack of height, and when some of my less energetic friends half-jokingly asked, 'When are you going to write about something that *we can do*?' the need became apparent. So I started checking and surprised myself with the quality and quantity of excellent shorter walks that can be found. A surprising number of them are little known.

The average altitude of this collection is 1500 ft (457m), average height gained is 1100ft (335m), average distance 4½ miles (7.2 km) and the average time just under three hours. All are 'rounds', enabling an easy return to the starting-point, including three which use lake steamer or miniature railway to complete the journey.

If your own favourite fell is not included that may be because I've already mentioned it in my first book referred to above. If it's not in there, then I apologise; I had to draw a line somewhere.

The Maps: All the walks can be found on the Ordnance Survey 1″ to the mile or 1:50,000 scale tourist maps of the Lake District and all except three of the walks (Black Combe, Whitbarrow Scar, Bowscale Fell) can also be found in more detail on the OS 1:25,000 scale Outdoor Leisure Maps, so the relevant one of those four is designated 'best map'. However, don't rely slavishly on the maps: footpaths which are clearly marked on the map may be hardly distinguishable on the ground (eg Cockley Beck to Red How) and there is an occasional footpath on the map that will lead you over a precipice on the ground.

Distances: These are not exact, simply approximations based on the map.

'Highest elevation reached' 'height gained': These are the actual heights in feet above sea level (converted to metres) from precise figures on the map if given; if not, the height is my best assessment.

The 'star rating': This is completely subjective. I have simply attempted to convey something of the overall quality of the walk. Fine mountain landscape and scenery and variety of interest are particularly important in this assessment. I know I have a definite

The Langdale Pikes seen from near Side Pike

preference for the wild places, the rough ground, the untracked rather than the smooth pathways and this will no doubt be obvious. I respond above all to fine landscape scenery. I go to the fells and mountains for exercise and recreation but I live for those moments when I just have to grab for my camera.

'**General level of exertion required**': On the whole the steeper the ascent, the greater the exertion. A short but steep climb can be a lot more exhausting than a long level stroll. I have simply attempted to give some indication of what to expect.

'**Time for the round**': My times are not based on any formula, but are an assessment based on my experience. They do *not* include lengthy lunch-stops.

'**Terrain**': In the introductory specifications for each walk I have added a few comments about the nature of the ground underfoot, which I hope will be helpful. Generally these refer to conditions in spring, summer or autumn; winter can introduce a new dimension of unpredictability which is the delight of experienced fellwalkers but could cause problems for beginners.

Clothing and footwear: The biggest cause of all accidents on the fells is slipping on wet grass and so the importance of suitable footwear – preferably warm, waterproof, well-fitting, giving support to the ankles and with suitably ridged soles – cannot be over-emphasised. Nor can I stress too strongly that

mild, balmy weather in the valley can be transformed at 1500 ft into something more like the Arctic. Wind- and waterproof clothing are essential except under the most settled conditions, and even then it's better to be safe than sorry. I personally swear by wool for each layer except my outer shell clothing, and I've tried everything.

Place names: In most cases, I believe I have used the spellings as on the relevant OS map, but there are minor alterations from one edition of those maps to another, and from one scale to another, so it will depend which edition of the 'relevant' map you are looking at. Usually there will be no problems at all in identifying the places concerned – i.e. Sour Milk Gill in Easedale and Sourmilk Gill in Easedale are obviously one and the same place; similarly, Hard Knott Pass is the same as Hardknott Pass. On the other hand, when a spike of rock on the side of Hard Knott (the fell, not the pass) is called The Steeple on one edition of the OS map and Eskdale Needle on another, that can cause confusion so I have tried to mention both. The other odd one is surely Esk Buttress in Upper Eskdale (a major rock-climbing crag and known as such to thousands of climbers for years) which the OS continues to call Dow Crag on the map. Here again I have used both names to avoid confusion.

Grid references: I have provided a grid reference for the starting point for each walk to help to begin from

The Dods from Castlerigg Circle, with the High Rigg ridge in the middle distance

the right place. The National Grid Reference System is explained in the bottom right-hand corner of all Ordnance Survey maps for anybody who isn't accustomed to using it.

Photography: After *On High Lakeland Fells* appeared, quite a number of people wrote expressing disappointment that I had not said more about the photographs. I don't really know what to say: I hardly ever use a tripod – I can't be bothered with its weight or the time it takes to set it up. All too often I see the shot I want just as the perfect light is vanishing and then hang around hopefully for it to reappear. I am prepared to 'stalk' my landscapes for a long time.

I have used Leica 35mm cameras for over twenty years and find that my present R4 reflex with 35mm–70mm zoom lens is the one I use now far more than any other because of the ease in altering format. So far as film is concerned, I used ASA 50 and 100 transparency film, my current favourite being Fujichrome.

View to Rannerdale Knotts from Crummock Water

PART ONE

Walks in the North-West

1. High Rigg

Best map: OS 1:25,000 N.W. Sheet (Ennerdale and Derwent)

Distance: Approx 4½ miles/7.2km

Highest elevation reached: 1163ft/354m

Height gained: 600ft/183m

Overall star rating: */* *

General level of exertion required: Fairly low

Time for the round: 2–2½ hours

Terrain: Firm, easy walking, though there may be boggy stretches on the return. A good all-weather walk, usually well below the cloud ceiling.

The ridge of High Rigg separates the main A591 Ambleside–Keswick road from the much quieter one going through the lovely St John's in the Vale and motorists on both rarely seem to have noticed it. Yet it is a fine, grassy ridge with rocky outcrops and splendid views of both Blencathra and Skiddaw.

Park in the National Trust car park at Legburthwaite, virtually opposite Castle Rock of Triermain on the Threlkeld – St John's in the Vale road (grid ref 318195), then make your way down a secondary road for a hundred yards which is reached by a gate from the car park to the main A591 itself. Just before it becomes dual carriageway, going towards Keswick, there is a ladder-stile over the wall on the right, beside a gate signed 'Public footpath St John's in the Vale, Churchbridge House'. Take the left fork in this path, heading upwards onto, not around, the toe of the ridge. A short climb through the trees discloses splendid views of two of Lakeland's rock playgrounds, Castle Rock of Triermain on the right and the equally imposing Raven Crag on the Thirlmere side of the main road. Continue pleasantly now, winding uphill through mature pine and oak trees until, as you leave the last of the pines, the broad-backed, hummocky ridge of High Rigg is reached, stretching invitingly ahead for a mile or more. This is of course the line of the walk. The hum of traffic will occasionally be heard, but the fine views along the whole of the ridge stretching from Clough Head to Great Dod, Stybarrow Dod and so to Helvellyn on the eastern side, with Skiddaw and Blencathra ahead to the north, are more than ample compensation.

The way is really very straightforward, following a well-defined path over the odd stile, through bracken and over short-cropped grass and although it appears

The ridge of High Rigg, with Skiddaw in the background

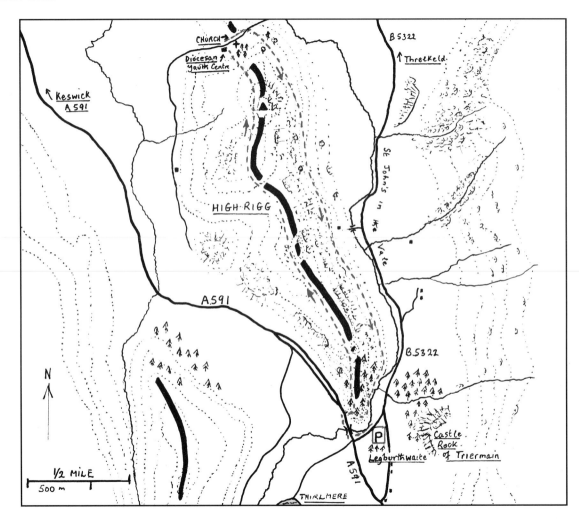

CHURCH

B 5322

↑ Threlkeld

Diocesan ↑
Youth Centre

↑ Keswick
A 591

St John's in the Vale

HIGH RIGG

A 591

B 5322

N
↑

Castle
Rook
of Triermain

Legburthwaite

A 591

½ MILE
500 m

THIRLMERE

to wander a little at times, attempts to take short cuts will only lead to unnecessary wall-climbing. The most distinctive of the high points seen in the near distance proves to be the little rocky summit of High Rigg and a good viewpoint.

After leaving the top, the path snakes down a grassy slope to reach a minor road, with the buildings of the Diocesan Youth Centre and the charming little church of St John's in the Vale, nestling among yew trees, only a few paces away on the pass. On early explorations, I tried to prolong this walk by continuing up the far slope of fields to reach the remainder of the ridge as it declines towards Tewet Tarn, but to get back without battling with walls and fences it is necessary to return the same way and it is not so attractive anyway. So turn eastwards on the road down the hill for a few yards to find the bridleway, signed to St John's in the Vale, on the right. If great tractor wheels haven't turned the first hundred paces into mud it will be an immediate pleasure to join the delightful grass track snaking across the fellside just outside the intake walls and slowly descending to the valley floor. Ignore tempting paths and tracks leading down towards the river and always keep to the right, until another good view of Castle Rock appears as the track approaches the water's edge. I feel certain there used to be a crossing here, over stepping-stones, which I used when I was doing the 'Lakeland Threes' some years ago (tops of 3000 ft and over), but I couldn't spot it last time I was there. Not that it matters for the path continues along the north bank

through tall larch woods, following the bend in the river, until the ladder-stile leading back to the main road appears again.

Blencathra seen from High Rigg

15

2. Nab Crags

Best Map: OS 1:25,000 N.W. Sheet (Ennerdale and Derwent)

Distance: 3 miles/4.8km, or double that for the longer walk to Ullscarf

Highest elevation reached: 1686ft/514m (or 2370ft/722m)

Height gained: 1100ft/335m or 1750ft/533m

Overall star rating: *

General level of exertion required: Medium; higher if you go to Ullscarf

Time for the round: 2 hours (or 3½ hours for the longer walk)

Terrain: A mixture of fair paths and rough, unmarked ground; not for inexperienced walkers. Not very suitable in misty weather at the higher levels.

This walk makes an effort to link some known paths, but it is really an exploration of some marvellously rugged and untrodden country. It can be a shortish walk or extended to take in the high top of Ullscarf, and it isn't easy to make into a good round; however, the ridge of Nab Crags should not be missed. This is clearly visible from the main road between Grasmere and Keswick at Wythburn, at the southern end of Thirlmere.

The best car park is the Forestry Commission one next to the bridge crossing Dob Gill at grid ref 316139. Ignore the signed coloured route-walks through the boring and view-restricting conifers, and walk along the road towards Wythburn for a little way and then take the first iron gate in the wall on the right. This leads to a stile and then a path uphill through heather and juniper to the left of the beck. This seeks the best line through the bushes, but climbs steadily and then trends back to the right to briefly enter the plantation over the forest-fence. Even if, like me, you're tempted to try to keep out of the woods, it is not advisable for the juniper really is impenetrable here: it's like Corsican maquis.

A forest track leads quickly to the outflow from the pretty Harrop Tarn – notable for its water-lilies and surround of trees and crags – but then turn left, over another stile and immediately another, to gain the open fell outside the forest and mostly above the juniper. A short climb beside a wall soon leads to a corner with a sheepfold, while from a grassy eminence on the left there are fine views down Thirlmere. Now go through the hurdle-gate beside the sheepfold and

Looking across Thirlmere to Nab Crags

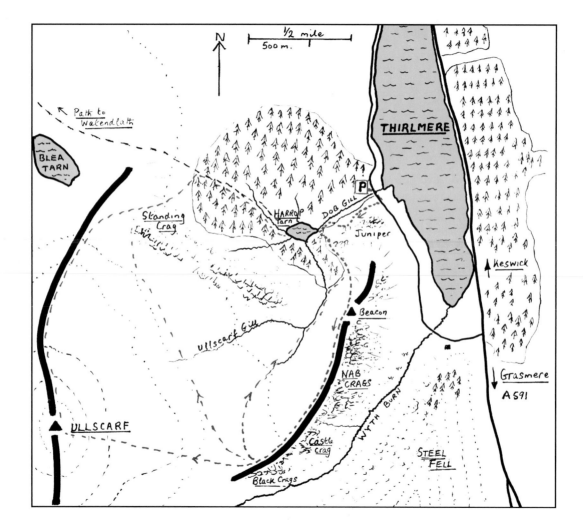

shortly afterwards through a slot in the wall on the left to make for a very prominent cairn or beacon, like a section of wall, which really marks the start of the Nab Crags ridge.

I first noticed this cairn properly nearly forty years ago when I tramped with a fifteen-year-old friend over these fells in pouring rain, got completely soaked (in the days when my waterproof was an oilskin cycle-cape), realised that we'd never get to Ambleside Youth Hostel that night and decided that a camp in the woods was the only choice left. Fortunately the rain stopped and we lit a huge fire (not approved by the Forestry Commission!) and shivered stark naked round it while our clothes dried, finally falling asleep exhausted in our little tent. Finding the forest edge and sighting that beacon the following morning gave us our bearings again.

Shortly after passing through the hurdle-gate and climbing up to the beacon, you have the delight of being up on the edge of this rocky scarp which leads steadily upwards along Castle Crag and Black Crags. It is just rocks, grass, bilberry, bog, wind and the occasional birdsong, with grand views to the side of Helvellyn that you normally never see and down the length of Thirlmere to Blencathra and Skiddaw. A moorland trudge – and it is a trudge, but you must have the rough sometimes to appreciate the smooth – now follows for the rest of the way to Ullscarf. The reward is good, but distant, views on a fine day to Bowfell, Gable and the Scafells, after which the fence-line leads down north-east to Standing Crag.

If the upward toil to Ullscarf is too much to contemplate, you may avoid it by some sideways toil instead, contouring across rough ground, listening to the skylarks and peewits and so reaching the same point. From here you should see the path from Watendlath leading towards the forest-fence and you can re-enter the boring conifers. The path is a bit vague in places but all the streams lead back to Harrop Tarn and so to the start. And if even sideways toil does not appeal, you can always go back down the way you came up.

Helvellyn and Thirlmere seen from near the beacon at the end of Nab Crags

3. Latrigg

Best Map: OS 1:25,000 N.W. Sheet (Ennerdale and Derwent)

Distance: 5 miles/8km

Highest elevation reached: 1203ft/367m

Height gained: 925ft/282m

Overall star rating: */* *

General level of exertion required: Medium/Low

Time for the round: 2–2½ hours

Terrain: Good paths and tracks over the whole distance

Latrigg is unquestionably dwarfed by Skiddaw which rises two thousand feet higher, for it lies at its base, in some respects like a rounded footstool. However, its ascent gives fine views over Keswick, Derwentwater and up Borrowdale and to walk over its top and return along the valley of the River Greta is of much greater interest and variety than I ever suspected. Because the paths are so good and the way so obvious (particularly if the straightforward return is made, rather than my option along the river bank) this is a very good family (or indifferent weather)

walk. In spring or autumn, when the trees can be a delight to see, it is doubly enjoyable.

The start is at grid ref 268242 at the end of Spooney Green Lane which is marked and well signed 'Public Bridleway to Skiddaw'. Cars can be parked on the roadside next to a small housing estate which is reached by following the A591 Carlisle road out of Keswick but turning right just after the hospital and before reaching the major roundabout where the road joins the A66. (The start is very close to the Keswick Spa leisure complex which is on the approximate site of the old railway station, so signs to the Spa – and to the station which are still about – may also be helpful.)

Spooney Green Lane leads rapidly to a bridge over the A66 then steadily upwards over several stiles and alongside a spruce plantation. If you stay with the main path alongside the forest you will curve gently round the flank of Latrigg and emerge – probably with a slight sense of irritation – not at a summit, but at a car park where other fell-walkers leave their vehicles before trudging off up the dreary track to Skiddaw via Jenkin Hill. You may be forgiven for thinking: 'Why on earth have I tramped about 700 feet up here when I could have driven up in the car in the first place?' Relax! There's better to come.

(If on the other hand you had spotted the grassy

Latrigg seen from the A591; Skiddaw is in shadow behind

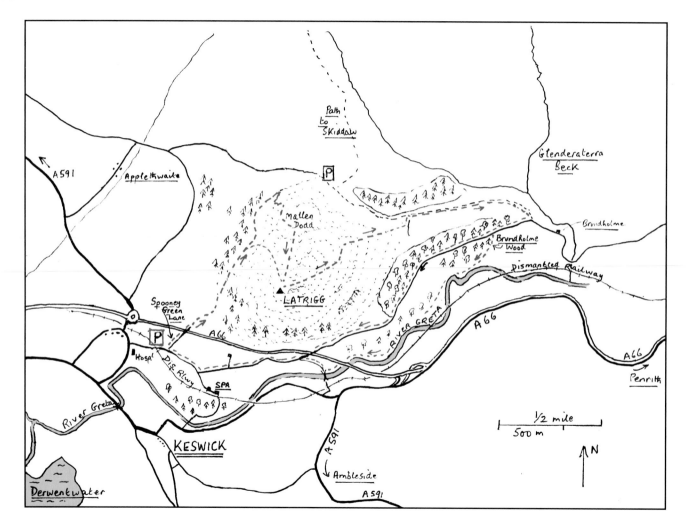

track heading off the main path to the right *before* you reached the Skiddaw car park, you could have zig-zagged quickly to the top of Mallen Dodd (a subsidiary top of Latrigg), not been aware of the car park and shortly arrived at the top of Latrigg itself.) Assuming however that, like me, you miss the direct way – or aren't sure enough of where you are going – and so reach the high-level car park on Latrigg's shoulder, you can always imagine that it isn't there and just walk south up another path across grassy moor to reach Latrigg's summit, from where you may admire the view.

When ready to leave, turn sharply north-east and follow the broad ridge-line towards the defile where the Glenderaterra Beck separates Skiddaw from Blencathra, crossing a stile in a wall, going through a gate and joining another old 'green road'; this leads rapidly to a metalled road, with gate and stile, at Brundholme.

A little further on the valley is crowded with river, road and defunct railway. Turn back right, along the minor metalled road, and head back towards Keswick, a simple and direct return. Though I personally hate walking along a yard more tarmac than is absolutely necessary, this is a very quiet lane indeed and more tolerable than most. However I do think it more interesting, though muddier in a wet season, to descend paths towards the River Greta (there are various places where this is possible). Then a water-side path leads through delightful mixed woodland along the banks of the broad stream, climbing at one

point to avoid shaly hillside above a great loop in the river, then passing under the huge and impressive viaduct carrying the A66, before descending to the river again at a bridge. Don't cross here but stay on the north bank and follow a pot-holed roadway climbing past a few houses and stables to rejoin the metalled lane that you forsook after descending to the long ridge from Latrigg earlier. This leads in ten minutes back to Spooney Green Lane and the start.

Cloud cap on Skiddaw, seen from the Latrigg path

4. Catbells and Derwentwater

Best Map: OS 1:25,000 N.W. Sheet (Ennerdale and Derwent)

Distance: 4 miles/6.4km approx.

Highest elevation reached: 1481ft/451m

Height gained: 1200ft/366m

Overall star rating: * * / * * *

General level of exertion required: Medium

Time for the round: 3 hours

Terrain: Good paths mostly on earth or grass. Can be a bit boggy in places near the edge of Derwentwater. All the higher-level walking is on well-marked paths on an obvious ridge.

I rediscovered Catbells just a few years ago, climbing it very early on a cold but brilliantly bright February morning, and have been back several times since then, once finding a beautiful return route that I hadn't known previously along the shores of Derwentwater. Don't let the fact that this is a 'popular' ascent put you off, or the details of trying to describe the way, for it is a lovely walk. Just try to pick a less popular time.

The best start is at Gutherscale (grid ref 246212) where there is a signed car park on the northern end of the Catbells ridge, between Hawes End and the farm at Skelgill, a couple of miles south of Portinscale. A sign points the way from the car park to the ridge, up a good path. As it climbs higher it zigzags up slaty shale, past (or round) an awkward place, over one bump and then up the first real hump on the ridge. Bracken slopes on the left stretch down to the Grange road, overlooking Derwentwater as height is gained, while to the right can be seen the amazingly green fields of Newlands and the peaks and ridges of the Derwent fells. Just left of the screes of Barrow is Farm Uzzicar and the spoil-heap of Barrow Mine which was very active a hundred years ago. (Apparently the farm itself is named after the tarn which was drained about six centuries ago to provide the 'new lands'. The ridge levels off for a short distance and then rears up again with a final rocky bit before the rounded summit at Catbells is reached.

Descend the ridge beyond, with good views across the head of Derwentwater to the cliffs of Falcon Crag, Shepherd's Crag and Black Crag, all standing guard over Borrowdale, and equally good views to the shapely fell of Hindscarth. Follow the path down to the col, Hause Gate, and descend on a good path, down steep zigzags, with railings here and there, until it is running alongside a wood. Complete the descent

The final slope up to Catbells from the north

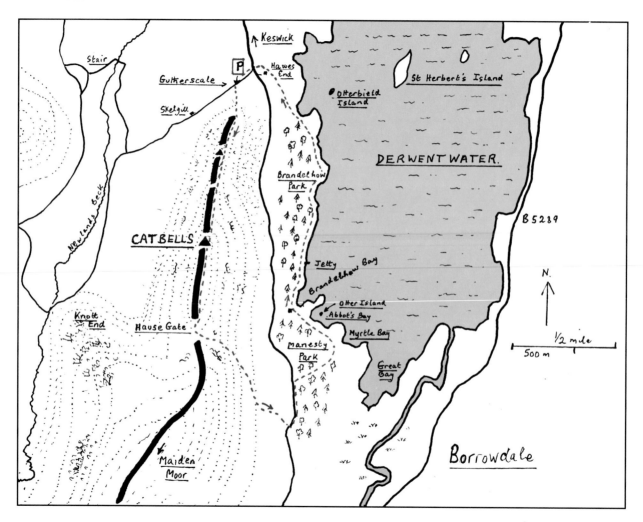

to a gate and stile and reach the road. Turn left along it for two hundred paces and then turn right, on the bend, at a sign 'Low Manesty', and follow the metalled track into the wood, which also hides a caravan park. Keep right at the first fork on the track, which leads through very attractive mature pine, birch and oak trees, and then turn right again through a gate (next to a five-barred one) in a wall leading out of the wood and towards the edge of Derwentwater at Myrtle Bay.

Here you join an attractive lakeside path which crosses some marshy land on stilts and then fairly quickly re-enters the wood through another gate, but now keeps closer to the water. The lakeside views are lovely, particularly from Abbot's Bay where the tiny Otter Island is covered in heather (the sheep can't get at it) and pine trees. The path now runs alongside a fence and meets a metalled track at a slate-built house ('The Warren'); here you turn right and follow several signs for Brandelhow, Hawes End and Keswick. Leaving the bay, now take the path through a gate into Brandelhow Wood where a jetty reaches into the lake. A delightful path leads through the wood at the water's edge for half a mile or so to another jetty at a wall with a gate. Beyond this, the path leads directly back towards the road, or you may choose to walk around the promontory ahead with its good views beyond the even tinier Otterbield Island. Either way, it is now just a short way back, along a track past an outdoor activities cottage, to the metalled road at the Hawes End Outdoor Activities Centre.

In a hundred paces turn off the road, up a path which cuts a corner round the end of the fell, to meet the road again on the bend just at the bottom of the Catbells ridge.

Newlands from the summit of Catbells

27

5. High Doat and Castle Crag

Best map: OS 1:25,000 N.W. Sheet (Ennerdale
and Derwent)

Distance: 4½ miles/7.2km

Highest elevation reached: 750ft/229m

Height gained: 500ft/152m

Overall star rating: * *

General level of exertion required: Fairly low.

Time for the round: 2–2½ hours

Terrain: Good paths, with the option of some
open fell on High Doat. If wet, the slate on
Castle Crag will need to be climbed with care.
This is a splendid half-day, off-day, wet-day or
family walk. If it's misty, however, don't
bother going onto High Doat.

Castle Crag is a prominent feature of the Borrowdale landscape, for its distinctive wooded mound almost fills the 'jaws' of Borrowdale and catches one's eye from several points while travelling south along Derwentwater. High Doat is not nearly so obvious, but it is a delightful, small fell, ideal for a peaceful picnic. Most people have never heard of it, which is why it's so undisturbed. This walk enables the two places to be linked, with a return through the beautiful Borrowdale woodland and beside the waters of the sparkling River Derwent.

Start in Seatoller where there is a large car park at grid ref 245138, and then walk up the Honister Pass road past Yew Tree Cottage. The first gated bridleway on the right marks the point at which the old Honister road begins its climb and this is the way to go. If you continue to the second, also gated, path just on the bend of the main road, you may climb fairly steeply and directly up the fell until a gate leads through the intake wall, at which turn right. Here a sudden and dramatic view of Castle Crag will shortly be seen ahead.

However, this more direct and perhaps more obvious way passes behind, and avoids, the delightful High Doat which is well worth visiting, so do take the old bridleway – the first gate – which starts by apparently heading east back down Borrowdale. This then leads through a farm gate and swings sharply back left, heading for Honister. Don't go left but continue straight ahead and now follow less obvious and grassy tracks, climbing steadily up the brackeny fellside, soon reaching the top of High Doat. This is an unspoilt and tranquil place for a short rest, a good viewpoint over Johnny Wood to the Watendlath

Castle Crag from the slopes of High Doat

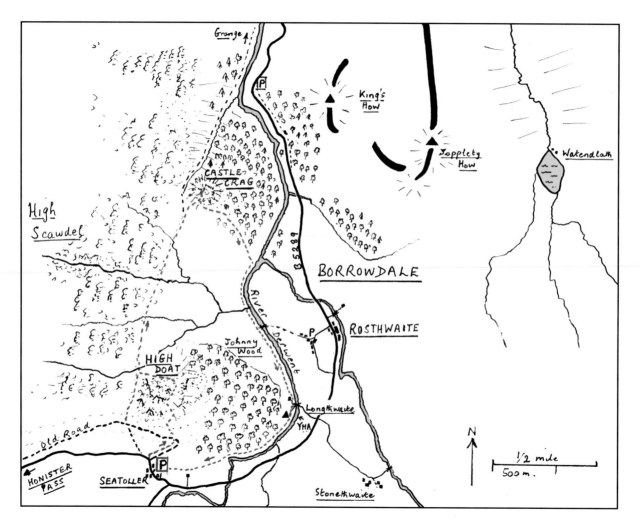

fells, and to Glaramara and the Scafell range to the south. It also gives a fine view of the main objective, Castle Crag itself.

Descend from High Doat in a curving line leftwards towards the obvious wall contouring High Scawdel, making use of the permissive path leading to a large stile. On its other side is the main track, leading towards Castle Crag and Grange, which is followed until it begins to lead downhill through the defile between Castle Crag and Low Scawdel. Now a narrower path leads off to the right, up a little rockier section, then over stiles through the larches, to finish steeply up the slate-spoil on to the top of Castle Crag itself, where there is a memorial to Borrowdale men who gave their lives in the Great War of 1914–18. It will have been obvious from the approach that the views from the summit are worth seeing – and they are, over the beautiful wooded country towards Derwentwater and southwards to the head of Borrowdale and the Scafell massif. Choose a quiet day and this can be an enchanting place to linger for a while.

To descend, reverse the last section of the slate path, then climb a stile and head south towards Rosthwaite and the green fields on the valley floor below. Johnny Wood is now the objective and is visible straight ahead as the path descends steeply through woodland, beside the wall; then along the right (west) bank of the River Derwent to meet the corner of the wood at Longthwaite.

Once past the Youth Hostel (here in a particularly beautiful setting), the path hugs the river bank again

as it passes alternately through and along the edge of this fine sessile oak wood and Seatoller is soon regained.

Looking south from near Manesty to Castle Crag

31

6.   Jopplety How and Brund Fell

Best Map: OS 1:25,000 N.W. Sheet (Ennerdale and Derwent)

Distance: 5½ miles/8.8km approx.

Highest elevation reached: 1363ft/415m

Height gained: 1100ft/335m

Overall star rating: * * *

General level of exertion required: Medium

Time for the round: 3½–4 hours

Terrain: Mostly on good paths but with some rocky and boggy sections on the open fell. In misty weather, you'll need confidence in your map-reading ability.

This is an excellent walk of continuous interest and variety, visiting the lovely wooded area of Lodore Falls, rising to the higher valley leading to Watendlath, climbing to some fine and rugged heights and descending through the woods of Troutdale.

The best parking is on the roadside near the Borrowdale Hotel (grid ref 262183), about four miles south of Keswick on the B5289, having passed alongside Derwentwater. If you take the footpath between the buildings of High Lodore Farm up Ladder Brow, you will only see the upper part of the Lodore Gorge. To see the lower falls, walk a little way back along the road to the Lodore Swiss Hotel, take the path round its back and cross the footbridge. Now follow the path through the trees, apparently climbing well away from the gorge but soon swinging back below the rock-climber's territory of Gowder Crag and up the left flank of the ravine. (Climbers beware: there's one place up there, where one has to sit to belay, which is surrounded by voracious little ants!) At the top, the river takes a sharp left bend and the track follows it at a higher level. Various short cuts can be made but they all lead to the same solid footbridge leading over to the other (west) bank of the Watendlath Beck.

The path now leads along the right bank of the beck towards Watendlath, up the almost level valley bounded by Grange Fell on the right and Ashness Fell on the left. This is a lovely stretch of the walk as there are open grassy swards and the trees are less confining. The odd knotted rope dangling from an overhanging branch shows where kids and their dads have fun swinging out over the water during summer picnics. Watendlath is soon reached by turning left over the packhorse bridge spanning the outflow from Watendlath Tarn. If it's not packed with tourists, this is a lovely place.

The approach to Watendlath via Watendlath Beck, with Grange Fell and Brund Fell beyond

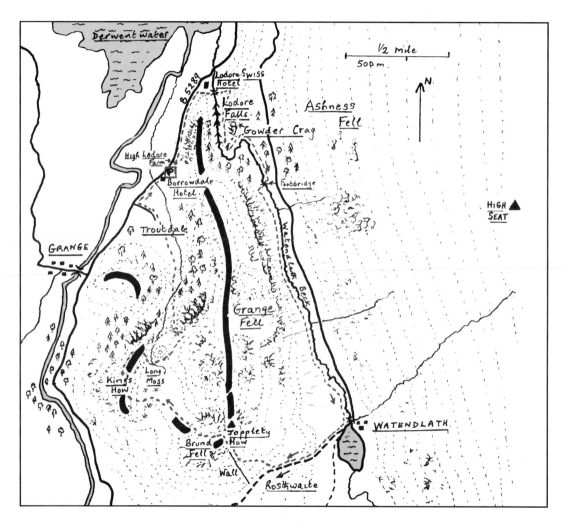

On leaving, cross the bridge again and climb the broad track south-west signed towards Rosthwaite, but not for too long for you are now off into wild country and the craggy little summits to the right (north) are the next objective. They are best reached by turning off the main track at the first path on the right and gaining a substantial stone wall running down the fellside. The path follows this wall and eventually over it to climb to the marvellous little summit of Jopplety How – a wonderfully named example of the rough, craggy, volcanic rock covered in nodules, fashioned into strange shapes and surrounded by heather that characterises this part of the Lakeland fells. I'm not absolutely sure which bit is Brund Fell but it's here somewhere too. You can find many completely peaceful and secret places here to sit and have your sandwich and watch the play of the light and shade over the surrounding fells. On a clear day, the views are outstanding.

Leaving the fell-tops, follow any of several paths through heather, downhill and initially westwards (towards Borrowdale). These all wander around rocky outcrops but, as you descend further, begin to choose those which lead north along the shoulder of the fell towards two more distinctive fell-tops. The path leads to a ladder-stile over a wall, then over a fence in the depression of Long Moss. Just ahead is the superb vantage point of King's How, easily gained by a short scramble and which shouldn't be missed. Now follow the wet path around the edge of the Moss, then wind down and into a stony gully amidst the trees at the head of Troutdale. This is steep but the path soon reaches a stile on the left bank of the gill and a final short descent leads to an almost level stroll through this delightful and enclosed little valley. All that remains is to go down the lane and turn right at the main road to return to the start.

On the descent from King's How to Troutdale

35

7. Great Crag

Best Map: OS 1:25,000 N.W. Sheet (Ennerdale and Derwent)

Distance: 5 miles/8km

Highest elevation reached: 1250ft/381m

Height gained: 1000ft/305m

Overall star rating: * *

General level of exertion required: Medium

Time for the round: 3 hours or so

Terrain: A mixture of good paths and rough fell with some boggy stretches. Good visibility desirable.

Great Crag is the highest bit of land to the immediate south-west of Watendlath and although the initial climb towards it is by a very popular path, the rest of this walk leads to a marvellous viewpoint amidst wonderful, wild fells. It looks nothing on the map; don't be misled, this is a splendid walk.

Start in Rosthwaite; there is a good, well-signed car park up a side road opposite the friendly post office and general store (grid ref. 258148). Then, back on the main road, take the metalled track over the river (signed 'Public Bridleway Stonethwaite/Watendlath') and go left along the path just outside the hotel grounds. (An attractive-looking path leads off to the right and this will be for the return.)

The path soon becomes more of a track climbing the fellside; it leads through a gate about halfway up, crosses the beck and then, as it levels out, reaches a wall with a five-barred gate. The main track continues to Watendlath, a charming hamlet that can be easily over-popular, but since you are made of sterner stuff and not to be tempted by thoughts of refreshment just yet, turn immediately you pass through the gate and go through another on the right.

A much less well-used path now leads towards open fellside, winding along just below the rim of the depression which holds Watendlath Tarn. The path skirts a little rocky height while making for a greater one which has a wall traversing it. You are not yet on the height of land but are crossing a moor, colonised by bog myrtle; here considerate walkers before you have tried to ease the way with flat stones across the wettest bits. The boggiest bit is reached when you meet a wire fence and gate and a discreet sign: 'To avoid damage to the wetland ahead and to conserve its wildlife please follow the waymarked route shown

View to Great Crag and the Watendlath Fells from the old Honister Pass road

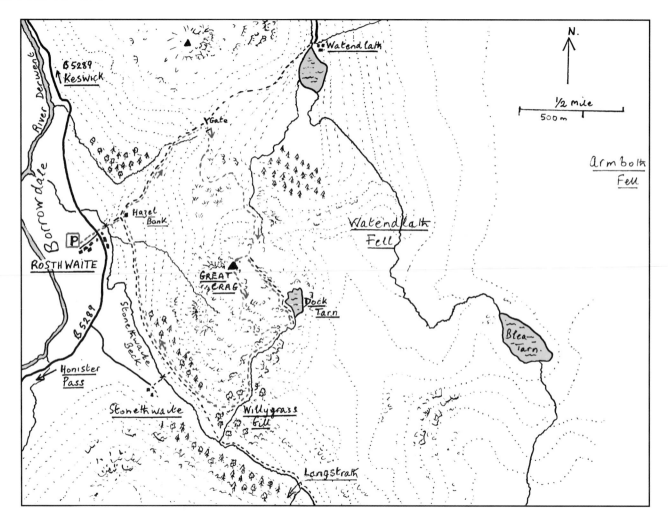

N.

½ mile
500 m

Watendlath

B 5289
Keswick
↑

Armboth
Fell

Gate

Watendlath
Fell

Hazel
Bank

P

ROSTHWAITE

GREAT
CRAG

Dock
Tarn

Blea
Tarn

Honister
Pass

B 5289

Stonethwaite Beck

Stonethwaite

Willygrass
Gill

Langstrath

by the posts'. We are all conservationists now, so follow the posts which circle the boggy land and quickly lead upwards again, giving retrospective views of Watendlath and its tarn.

Now the way becomes firmer. Go through the wall by a kissing-gate and climb steeply beside the beck onto high heather-covered moorland – a fine sight when in bloom – with many outcrops of knobbly volcanic rock jutting through it. The path itself skirts under the highest ground so that if you stay on it you will simply trudge past the finest view. Turn right just before reaching a tall 'finger-post' of rock beside the path and go up a very faint path through thick heather to a cairn on the highest point, which is Great Crag. Compared with other 'Greats' in Lakeland, this one is a tiddler, but it is set amidst a marvellously wild and rugged volcanic landscape, with fine views both up and down Borrowdale.

The glint of water – Dock Tarn – can be seen nearly half a mile away to the south-east and the path you left leads to and skirts its near shore. But it is a reedy sheet of water and I think it is much better now to stay on the high ground as long as you can, heading south towards Langstrath. You will wind over and round more of these splendid rocky outcrops between the heather and the little passageways cropped short by the ever-hungry sheep, until you meet the main path again as it now leads away from Dock Tarn. This path descends the northern bank of Willygrass Gill towards Borrowdale, veering away from it as it steepens a little, going over a stile and then descend-

ing steeply in zigzags through a mature sessile oak wood to the green fields in the valley below.

Turn right as you reach the valley floor and soon you are opposite the lovely hamlet of Stonethwaite; then continue along the bridleway on the right (north) bank of the Stonethwaite Beck for a pleasant half mile or so. You are soon back in Rosthwaite.

Eagle Crag seen from Willygrass Gill on the descent from Dock Tarn

8. Barrow and Outerside

Best Map: OS 1:25,000 N.W. Sheet (Ennerdale
    and Derwent)

Distance: 4½ miles/7.2km approx

Highest elevation reached: 1863ft/568m

Height gained: 1500ft/457m

Overall star rating: *

General level of exertion required: Medium

Time for the round: 2–3 hours

Terrain: A good path to Barrow and Barrow Door
    (an easy escape here).
    Thereafter mostly an open but easy fell with just
    a few sheep tracks.

Barrow and Outerside are minor, but not insignificant, fells enclosed by the ridges of Coledale. Indeed, the distinctive shape and inviting ridge of Barrow, seen on the approach to Braithwaite and the Whinlatter pass from Keswick, catch the fellwalker's eye almost as much as the higher one of Causey Pike. Outerside is largely hidden from this angle but is higher and a fine fell in its own right. Just because they are not part of the Coledale skyline they are relatively unvisited, especially Outerside, and that is part of their attraction, for me anyway.

Start from Braithwaite (grid ref. 232235), a couple of miles west of Keswick, where there are few obvious car parks but lots of little odd corners. Walk out of the village on the road signed for 'Newlands', cross the bridge and take the track signed 'Public Bridleway Stair'. The track leads to a farm, through gates and past cow byres, through the last opening in the intake wall and up the field towards a wood on the hause and a finger-post sign. The main path over the hause continues to Stair, but go now directly up the well-defined grassy ridge of Barrow, with incut footsteps made in the turf by earlier peak-baggers showing the way. It is a straightforward climb – my ten-year-old son went up it faster than me – to the little pile of stones on Barrow's summit. There are excellent views: Causey Pike, Sail, Crag Hill and Grisedale Pike are all well seen from here.

After descending to the pass called Barrow Door, between Barrow and the grassy fell of Stile End, a well-marked track curves round the south flank of Outerside and the path from Barrow Door goes to join it. On the occasion I was walking with my wife and son, the wind and the rain arrived, and while they took the escape route from Barrow Door back to

*Blencathra and Keswick
from Barrow*

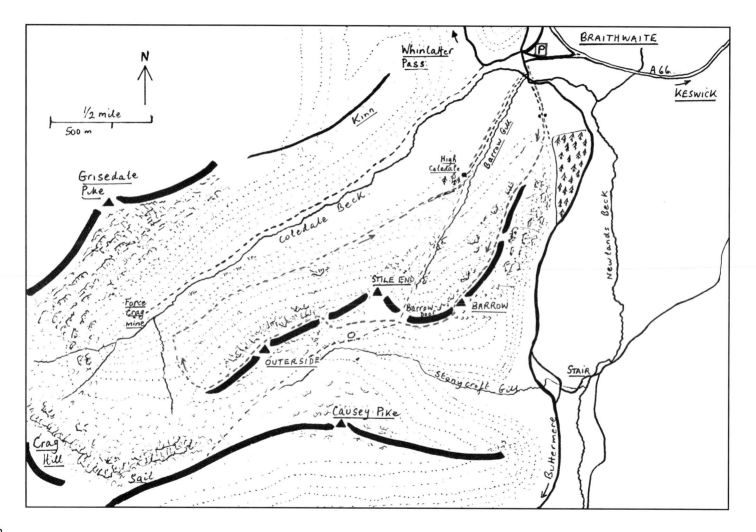

Braithwaite, I pressed on. Just before reaching the main path ahead, a sheepfold is passed on the right, built on some particularly boggy ground. It is obvious that by striking to the right here, up rough fellside and through tough heather for a short way, the hause between Stile End and Outerside – and the ridge up the latter – can be easily reached. I gained the hause and started up the ridge as the sky turned black and curtains of rain, driven by a howling wind, swept across the flanks of Grisedale Pike. Then the rain turned to sleet, the sleet to snow, the dogs tripped me up as they sheltered behind my legs from the blast, and I was in danger of being blown off the ridge. There wasn't another soul to be seen. But it was exhilarating to be battling with the elements, fighting to get to the top. I loved it – and I reached the top! Then the snow turned to sleet, visibility improved, and two scramble-motorbikes churned a wavering track up the opposite slope towards me, stalled their engines, restarted them and set off down towards Stonycroft Gill, disappearing into a mist. I'm not sure whether they heard the rather basic Anglo-Saxon language that followed them, noisy things.

There is definitely a path of sorts on the ridge and over the top as you descend towards the head of Coledale, but it soon disappears as the ridge flattens off into moor and it is not so obvious which way to go. Turn down the fellside, trending to the right away from the Force Crag mineworkings. The track to the mine is obvious enough on the other bank of the Coledale Beck, giving a fast but boring tramp, but

there's no necessity to batter your feet on the hard road. As you descend, look carefully for a level sheep-track, about two hundred yards up from the beck on the slope that you are on. Once found, this leads unerringly along Outerside's northern flank towards Braithwaite, becomes more of a path as it reaches the clump of trees at High Coledale and, with a final metalled lane, leads straight into the village.

View from Barrow to Outerside, with Causey Pike, Sail and Crag Hill on the left

9. Sale Fell

Best Map: OS 1:50,000 1¼″ to 1 mile (2cm to 1km) Landranger Sheet 90 (Penrith & Keswick). (Only partly on 1:25,000)

Distance: 2 miles/3.2km approx.

Highest elevation reached: 1170ft/357m

Height gained: 850ft/259m

Overall star rating: *

General level of exertion required: Low/Medium

Time for the round: 1½ hours

Terrain: Easy going on paths or grassy fell.

Sale Fell is at the northern end of Bassenthwaite Lake (the only 'lake' in the Lake District, the others all being 'meres' or 'waters'), a round little lump with a higher and a lower top. It is mostly hidden by the Wythop Woods as one travels along the Keswick–Cockermouth road beside the lake, but it is very apparent once you are round the corner and heading west. Its ascent is straightforward, unspoilt and one of the shortest and easiest in this book. It leads to several good viewpoints over Bassenthwaite, gives a steady climb on easy ground well away from the usual busy tracks on the more central fells and is an ideal family walk – or for dodderers of all ages.

Follow the A66 along the west bank of Bassenthwaite towards Cockermouth and, just beyond the dual carriageway section, turn off at the signs for Wythop Mill and The Pheasant Inn. There's good parking on the roadside near St Margaret's Church outside the hamlet (grid ref. 190301).

Walk back eastwards for about a hundred and fifty yards to where a sign 'Public Footpath Kelsick' points to a slanting track trending to the right across the grassy fellside and through a gate in the wall. In fifty yards more, it joins another green way (which I'm told encircles the fell, though I haven't tried it because I can't understand anyone other than a farmer wanting to walk round a fell and not go up it). Keep going right, gently uphill, until the green way runs alongside another wall and curves over the broad end of a long ridge leading leftwards towards higher ground. Now is the moment for an adventurous leap into the unknown. Leave the track here and instead head up the gently angled and grassy ridge itself. The leap is not too great for there is a fairly obvious line to follow, either up the crest of the ridge or on another grassy path which soon appears. Either leads easily to

Looking towards Skiddaw from Sale Fell

45

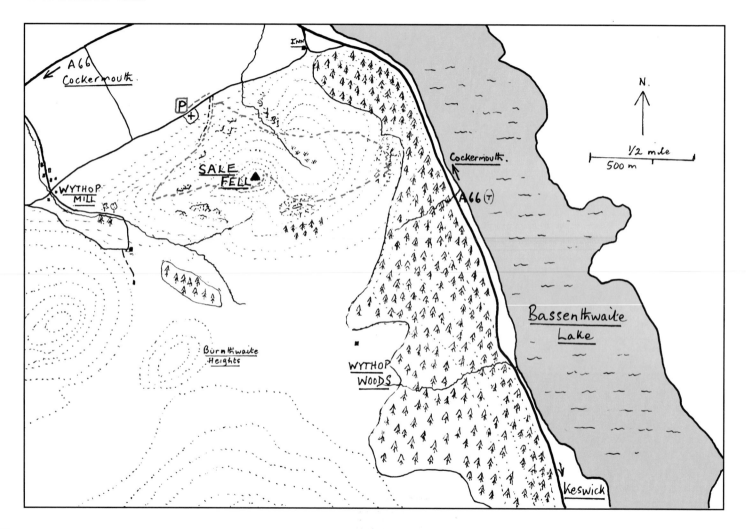

the twin rounded summits where there are a few rocks and probably a few sheep. Tractor marks on the ground indicate that it's easy enough for them to get up here and my son thought it easy enough to roly-poly downhill for a good distance.

There are views to Skiddaw over the Ullock Pike ridge, but Bassenthwaite Lake only shows as a tiny glint of water round a corner of the wood that clothes the western flank of the fell and it is better to wander over to the other rounded top for improved views. To get there, head towards Skiddaw, over firm grass and two collapsed walls to another cairn and then, veering left a little, reach the other top from where there are full-length views down the lake.

Keep swinging left now, towards the wall enclosing the forest, where its edge overlaps a shoulder of the fell, but before reaching it turn left along a sheep-track which skirts a reedy bog fringed with alders. A beck rises from the bog, flowing northwards, and a path soon develops and follows it, crossing over to the other bank before the waters begin the steeper descent down a gill. This leads to a green path which slants away from the gill, across the fell and soon reaches the fell-gate near the church again. It is all very straightforward and, despite being short, has much to offer.

As a pleasant end to this very easy and peaceful climb, why not wander around the churchyard with its mature yews. The roofs of its two fine lych-gates are covered with cotoneasters that look as though they've been there for centuries.

Bassenthwaite from the lower slopes of Sale Fell

47

10. Mellbreak

Best Map: OS 1:25,000 N.W. Sheet (Ennerdale and Derwent)

Distance: 5 miles/8km approx.

Highest elevation reached: 1676ft/511m

Height gained: 1300ft/396m

Overall star rating: * *

General level of exertion required: Medium

Time for the round: About 3 hours

Terrain: Mostly on fair paths over grassy fells, though there is no obvious descent path. Boggy in places along the shore of Crummock Water.

Mellbreak forms Crummock Water's west retaining wall but stands quite separate from nearby fells, with two tops. Seen from near Loweswater, its northern end is a sharp cone fringed by crags and a sporting way climbs up through these to the first summit. Crummock Water is in many respects as lovely as Buttermere but its circuit is a seven-mile walk and too much of that is on, or very near, the tarmac. So this walk climbs and traverses Mellbreak and then, in a delightful ramble, returns along the western shore of the lake where there are only sketchy paths, wonderful views and no tarmac or cars. It's a walk for the connoisseur.

The start is at Loweswater Church and the best and virtually only car parking near there is at the Kirkstile Inn situated most conveniently next to the church (grid ref 141209). (There is an alternative public car park in the wood by Scalehill Bridge (grid ref. 149215) and, if this one is used, just walk the extra few hundred yards along the quiet road to the church.) From the car park, Mellbreak's steep pike is directly behind the inn, so make for it by leaving along the metalled track which swings right and immediately crosses Park Beck. Once past the nearby farm buildings the road becomes a bridleway, twisting between stone walls, heading for one of the many Mosedales to the west of Mellbreak. You don't want to go too far in that direction so, when the bridleway swings right at a gate in front of a stand of larches, take instead the footpath leading directly up the firebreak and cut off the corner.

This path now climbs upwards across grass on the lower slopes of Mellbreak and can be seen rising in zigzags up the steeper fell ahead. It slants up scree, climbs a fine little rock rib, goes up a trench through the heather, then, finally rising above the parapet of

Mellbreak seen from Loweswater

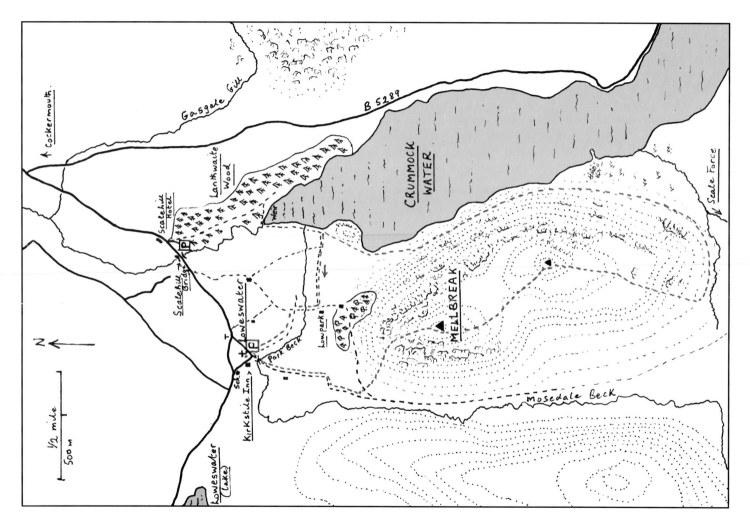

defending crags, reaches the shoulder of the fell. From here there is a good view along the length of Crummock Water towards Buttermere and an equally good one of the more pastoral scenery around Loweswater.

Go a little further at an easier angle and the first top is reached. After the summit cairn the path continues, but becoming sketchier, across heather moorland, down a depression and then up to a second summit. Continue down the fellside beyond, towards the tree-girt gorge of Scale Force which can be seen ahead across the valley, cleaving the flank of Starling Dodd on the High Stile ridge. There is no path down this end of the fell but it is easy walking and interesting to see the sheep-tracks contouring round it: I counted ten, each one about fifty feet higher than the last. I also nearly fell off the rock on which I was standing whilst counting as, with a sudden and intensely loud roar, two RAF trainer jets hurtled along the valley at a lower altitude than I was myself. My dogs cowered; the few sheep scattered and even a large dung-beetle dived for cover.

Grassy spurs down the slopes ahead now lead quickly to a footpath alongside Crummock Water. The way is certainly very wet in places where streams drain from the slopes above, but the views along the length of the valley, enhanced by little bays and the sparkling waters of the lake, are exceptionally fine. Nearing the northern end of the lake, the path leads to a stile and then round a lovely bay with a shingle beach. If you parked near Scalehill Bridge just keep going now to a footbridge over the outlet of the lake

and a track back through Lanthwaite Wood. If you parked near the church, swing left now to Lowpark, then a left turn at the minor road and five more minutes sees you back to the start.

Gasgale Crags and Grasmoor seen across Crummock Water

51

11. Carling Knott and Holme Wood

Best Map: OS 1:25,000 N.W. Sheet (Ennerdale and Derwent)

Distance: Low-level walk: 5½ miles/8.8km; High-level walk: 7½ miles/12km

Highest elevation reached: 500ft/152m (or 1675ft/510m

Height gained: 400ft/122m (or 1400ft/427m)

Overall star rating: * *

General level of exertion required: Low for the low-level walk, and medium-high for the high-level walk

Time for the round: 2½ hours (or 4 for the high route)

Terrain: Good paths and tracks (though a few sloppy places) on the low-level walk which is an excellent all-weather round. Tough and trackless on the high-level route where it climbs on to the open fell.

Lying north-west of Crummock Water, Loweswater is an attractive small lake, with a fine, mature wood on its western shore. Carling Knott is the shapely fell, rising a further 1000ft/305m above the tree line behind the wood. The best parking for both versions of this walk is at grid ref. 134210. This point is down a metalled track on the west side and about half way along the minor road between Loweswater lake and Loweswater hamlet. This track continues further to Watergate Farm but the parking is at the point where a second track leads off this one to High Nook Farm.

Start by taking the track signed to High Nook Farm, with Highnook Beck chattering on your left. Go through the yard and follow the track which is now up the left bank of the stream. Immediately beyond the fell-gate, take the right fork of the track towards the head of the valley, cross the beck by a footbridge and then double back on the other side, northwards, towards Loweswater. This is the low-level way and it climbs gently towards the shoulder of Carling Knott and then contours just outside the confines of Holme Wood. It is a delightful stretch of the walk, for not only do you overlook Loweswater but also the wood itself, of mature mixed conifer and deciduous trees which form a wonderful mosaic of colour and texture, especially in spring and autumn. Shortly after crossing Holme Beck, the path leaves the wood and then gently descends towards Fangs Brow Farm. Somewhere along here, though probably

Carling Knott and Holme Wood seen across Loweswater

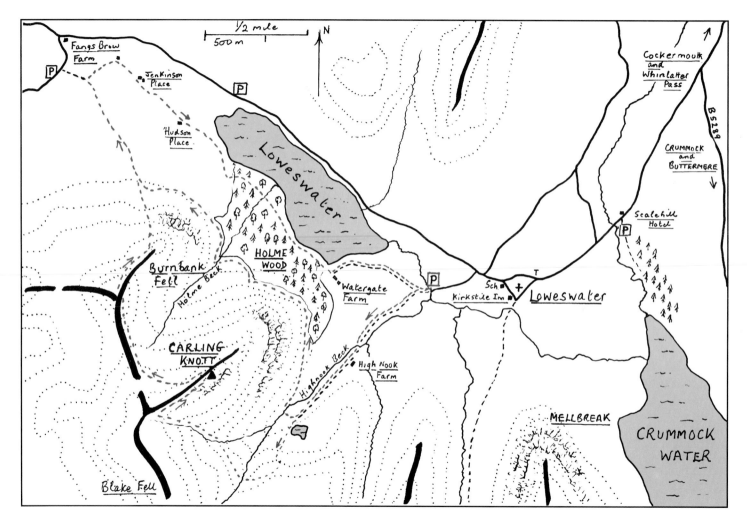

an hour or so later, those tough souls who have tackled Carling Knott will rejoin the walk.

For the alternative, having walked towards the head of the valley, go straight on, past a small tarn, through two stone gateposts in a non-existent fence, and then directly up the grassy spur defined by the beck on each side of it. This leads steeply through bilberry and without benefit of paths. As you gain height, desert the spur and climb the right-hand branch of Highnook Beck, following it to the watershed between Blake Fell and Carling Knott. Don't tackle the slopes of Carling Knott directly for the whole hillside is covered in tough heather at a steep angle.

From here it is a straightforward walk out to the highest point on Carling Knott where there's not much more than a few rocks and probably a few sheep, but it is the top. The views are better, however, when you've returned to the col and walked over trackless fell to the top of Burnbank Fell where a collection of rusty and twisted iron fencing embellishes the corner fence-post. Now head north-east along the broad back of the fell until you are overlooking Loweswater and can see the footpath below heading for Fangs Brow Farm. Choose the easiest line until you join the path. The two walks have now joined up again.

Just before reaching the road, turn right at a stile and take the delightful green track that follows the wall, curving round towards Loweswater. Past Jenkinson Place, the way becomes a path slanting down the

fields until it becomes a liquid mire as it dodges round Hudson Place, and then joins another bridleway leading almost to the edge of Loweswater. This stretch is now on the level, alongside the lake and then pleasantly through the edge of Holme Wood until Watergate Farm is reached. A short walk along the farm track returns you to your car.

Carling Knott seen across Crummock Water

12.   Rannerdale Knotts

Best Map: OS 1:25,000 N.W. Sheet (Ennerdale
    and Derwent)

Distance: 2½ miles/4km approx.

Highest elevation reached: 1160ft/353m

Height gained: 850ft/259m

Overall star rating: * *

General level of exertion required: Medium

Time for the round: About 2 hours

Terrain: A steep ascent on a fair path up grass,
    thereafter on good paths.

Rannerdale Knotts form a steep and rocky promontory jutting into the eastern side of Crummock
Water and the ascent, together with the traverse of
the ridge of Low Bank beyond and a return down
Rannerdale itself, is a short but delightful excursion.
It's perfect for a quick burst of exercise even in poor
weather, or for a more leisurely amble and ramble on a
fine day.

The road along the eastern side of Crummock
Water has a distinct kink in it where it forces through
the narrow gap between water and steep fellside at
Hause Point, but there is convenient parking directly
below steep crags about 200 yards south of Rannerdale
Farm (grid ref. 162183).

The craggy front is much too steep for direct ascent
but a green path rises almost from the parking area
towards a shoulder of the fell (in the opposite direction from the footpath sign pointing up Rannerdale).
This green path climbs to the right to a point
overlooking the lake and then becomes a line of
footsteps kicked into the turf, heading back left and
finally leading directly up to the rocky little summit
ridge. This is curiously named Low Bank but it is high
enough to be a splendid viewpoint for Grasmoor, for
Mellbreak seen from here across Crummock Water,
and indeed for the whole of the Buttermere valley.

Others must feel so. I finally decided that the grey
dust I saw sprinkled up there one day – and which I
puzzled over for a little while – must have been the
ashes of some other romantic fell-wanderer who had
hung up his boots for the last time and hoped his spirit
would be able to wander freely where he used to do so
himself . . .

The ridge now projects ahead, almost level, and
becomes quite rocky for some distance, then gently
descends along a green path, all the time overlooking
the lovely hamlet of Buttermere below. After a while

*Rannerdale Knotts seen
across Crummock Water*

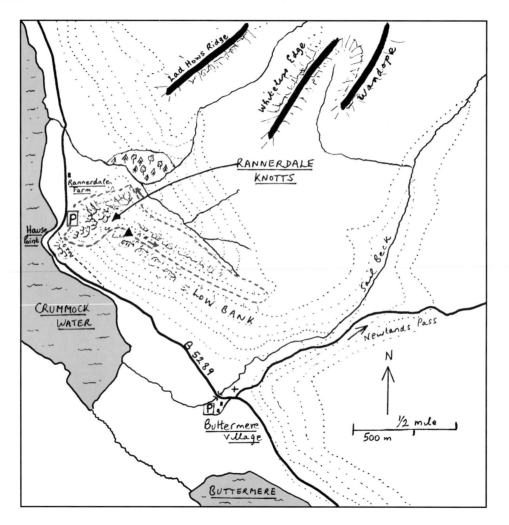

Crummock Water and Buttermere Fells seen from a shoulder on Rannerdale Knotts

a path heads off to the right, descending to Buttermere, but stay on the higher ground to reach the hause overlooking the Newlands Pass road as it climbs from Buttermere on its way to Braithwaite and Keswick. Another path goes uphill from the hause, zigzagging steeply up the fellside towards Wandope and Grasmoor, but turn sharply left now, down Rannerdale on another green pathway. This leads very pleasantly down the dale and over the intake wall by a large ladder-stile. Don't cross the footbridge over the beck but follow the path down the left bank alongside the tumbling waters, then, as Rannerdale Farm comes into view, swing left outside the field wall to return, via one kissing-gate, to the parking place.

13.   Green Crag and Haystacks

Best Map: OS 1:25,000 N.W. Sheet (Ennerdale and Derwent)

Distance: 5 miles/8km approx.

Highest elevation reached: 1860ft/567m

Height gained: 1450ft/442m.

Overall star rating: * * *

General level of exertion required: Medium/high

Time for the round: 3½ hours

Terrain: On straightforward though sometimes very rocky paths and care may be required on the descent from Haystacks.

The traverse of Haystacks is a justifiably popular expedition, with a fine variety of scenery, from verdant sheep pastures to rough rocky tops that would not be out of place on Scafell. Good visibility is not essential because the way is well marked, except under new snow.

The best start is at Gatesgarth Farm at the bottom of Honister Pass on the Buttermere side (grid ref. 196150). From here, walk back up the road a short way and then take the almost level track which skirts

under the north ridge of Fleetwith Pike, leading into the cirque of Warnscale Bottom. It is surprising how quickly you enter another world, even on a busy weekend, as you head into this combe – although I have never known it so quiet as when I walked this way one mid-week day, and had a most unusual experience.

I was completely alone with my two dogs and heard a strange noise which I soon saw was being caused by a fox who was leaping up onto the intake wall and then leaping off again. As I drew closer, I saw that he was in fact caught by a wire round his body and he wasn't so much jumping off the wall as being pulled back by the wire when he tried to jump over it. As I got nearer, he shot into the hogget-hole at the base of the wall where he lay, nose showing, tugging frantically at the wire. I know farmers consider the fox to be an enemy and I quite agree that they need to be controlled: I've seen the damage a fox can do to a pen of chickens. But this was November and not lambing time. There was no way that I could let him just rot there on the end of a wire (which I'm certain he'd got into by accident), nor could I go and find the farmer who would probably shoot him. So, with some trepidation, I admit, I tied up my dogs and very carefully found a joint, where a thicker wire was joined to the thinner one which held the fox, and released him. For

Green Crag and Haystacks, seen from Buttermere

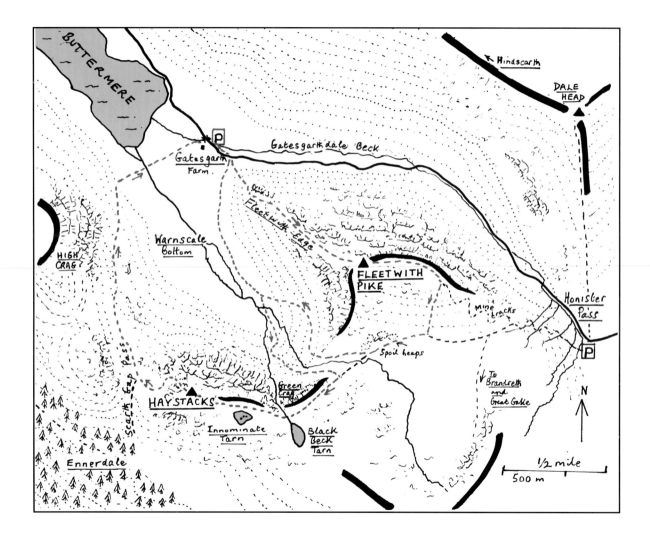

BUTTERMERE

← Hindscarth

DALE
HEAD

P

Gatesgarthdale Beck

Gatesgarth
Farm

grass

Fleetwith Edge

Warnscale
Bottom

HIGH
CRAG

FLEETWITH
PIKE

mine tracks

Spoil heaps

Scarth Gap Pass

Green
Crag

To
Brandreth
and
Great Gable

HAYSTACKS

Innominate
Tarn

Black
Beck
Tarn

Honister
Pass

P

N

Ennerdale

½ mile

500 m

a few seconds he didn't move. Then he shot off like a bullet from a gun and quickly vanished. By now the mist was down on Haystacks, but I completed my round with a much lighter heart.

Walking into Warnscale Bottom, the steep cliffs of Green Crag are directly in front, while to the right the face of Haystacks is seamed with sunless clefts that have steep screes below them. Nowadays it seems extraordinary that early pioneers of rock-climbing like Oppenheimer should have seen these frowning gullies as tempting places for early rock-climbing exploration. But who knows, their day may come again.

A stony bridleway winds across the left-hand slope but it is more interesting to follow the green path that can be seen rising up the fellside below Green Crag itself and is reached over a footbridge. The path curves out to the right and then back, well below the great gullies and passing just below a little stone building – half of it renovated to form a bothy – and allows a much better view of the gorge down which the stream tumbles, before it joins the much broader path on the ridge-top coming from Honister Pass. Don't take the left fork, which goes off to Brandreth, but keep right, behind Green Crag, descending to Black Beck just below the outlet from the tarn of the same name. Now it slants up round the rocky flank of Haystacks and quickly reaches the lovely Innominate Tarn with its three rock islands. From here the main path climbs steadily, via a series of rocky steps, to the summit of Haystacks, although I prefer to wander along the crinkly edges of the great gills and look out

over the void to Buttermere and Crummock. On the summit itself an old iron fence-post is still embedded in the rock and a tiny tarn glints only a few feet lower.

To descend, follow the line pointed out by three more posts, then, after the fourth, follow cairns which swing well to the left and lead by rocky steps to the foot of a gully. Beyond lie more open screes; you are below the defences and can now go more easily down to the top of the Scarth Gap Pass. Simply follow the path back down to Gatesgarth. What a splendid round!

Haystacks from the slopes of Fleetwith Pike

14. Fleetwith Pike

Best Map: OS 1:25,000 N.W. Sheet (Ennerdale and Derwent)

Distance: 3 miles/4.8km approx.

Highest elevation reached: 2136ft/651m

Height gained: 1700ft/518m

Overall star rating: * *

General level of exertion required: Quite high

Time for the round: 2½ hours

Terrain: A good path, with some easy scrambling, on the uphill stretch when you need it, and also on the descent, which you can vary at will. There should be no particular problems even in misty weather. Even when you can see very little, there's a lot of retrospective pleasure to be gained once you're warm and dry again . . .

I pondered for some time as to whether Fleetwith Pike really fits into this collection of 'lower fells', but there are four good reasons for inclusion: it has such a fine north-west ridge, it does stand essentially alone, it is only a couple of hundred feet higher than many others in this book and it gives such a very satisfying short round.

There is good parking at Gatesgarth Farm at the bottom of Honister Pass close to Buttermere (grid ref. 196150). The ridge of Fleetwith Edge dominates the skyline to the south-east, forming the right-flanking wall of Honister Pass as seen from here. An obvious path leads straight from the road towards the ridge where a white memorial cross is visible just below steeper crags. This path climbs quickly, but soon reaches an eroded section on the flank, which is more pleasantly by-passed by zigzagging further right up the line of the ridge itself. You'll soon rejoin the main path at the top of this first steep section where it is comparatively level for a short way; then strike upwards again, leaving the bracken behind and winding up through an area of heather and bilberry, with an occasional steeper and rockier bit to climb.

At a second shoulder, the grass takes over and the angle is easier again, though it soon leads into a longer final section, having several little rock-scrambles on the way and with more heather than bilberry on each side. The views down the full length of Buttermere and Crummock can be very impressive from several vantage points on this ascent and you'll

Buttermere and Crummock Water seen from Fleetwith Pike

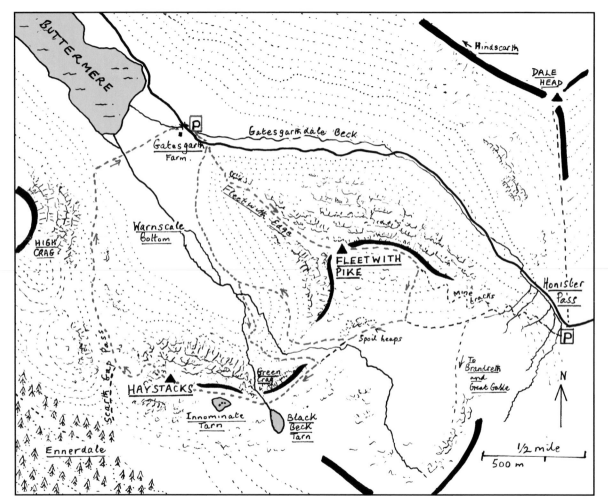

be sure to be glad to pause and admire them . . . Reaching the summit-cairn, of course, gives another justifiable excuse to collapse and consume your sandwiches. You may get a view to Great Gable and even to the Scafells.

Next follow the ridge which stretches away over rocky ground towards Honister Pass itself. The hard uphill work is now over; you are virtually on the level and there are marvellous views down the defile of the pass.

Just beyond the highest point, marked by a cairn, some old buildings will be seen hidden in a former quarry scooped out of the ridge itself. Take the path which starts to swing right here, heading for the hause where the broad track to Brandreth and Great Gable can be seen. Once a rusty old iron hut is reached, swing right onto the main path. This is a former bridleway to and from old workings whose remains are to be found at the junction with the path to Haystacks amid some huge slate spoil-heaps, and where one of the old buildings has been a climbing-club's hut for years. This track runs just above a fine gorge with a waterfall, before swinging away well to the right in a gradual descent which will lead steadily, though bone-shakingly, down to Gatesgarth again.

Personally, I prefer to leave the bridleway where it goes right and follow the right edge of the ravine down broken little ribs of rock to reach the water. The stream can be crossed on large boulders and the descent continued down the left bank, over rocky steps and grass rakes, close to several fine little

waterfalls otherwise missed, joining the last of the zigzags for the final descent.

The beck has to be crossed again to rejoin the main track, but this time there is a footbridge and it is now only a gentle stroll past a plantation of pines to Gatesgarth Farm again.

View to the north-west ridge of Fleetwith Pike from Crummock Water

15.   Circuit of Buttermere

Best Map: OS 1:25,000 N.W. Sheet (Ennerdale and Derwent)

Distance: 4½ miles/7.2km approx.

Highest elevation reached: 400ft/122m

Height gained: negligible

Overall star rating: **

General level of exertion required: Very low

Time for the round: 2 – 2½ hours

Terrain: Easy and virtually level walking. I have met dads with push-chairs on this round, but they must have carried the push-chairs (and infants) at least a little of the way.

Despite the comparative ease of this walk and the fact that it has been a popular round for at least a hundred years, it really is a most beautiful circuit of a lovely lake ringed by superb fells. For a leisurely stroll on a fine day, or a couple of hours' exercise on a wet or misty one, it is still an experience not to be missed. Personally, I wouldn't choose a gloriously fine day for it because there are always more demanding things to be done then, but I can see a day in the future when I will hardly be able to set one foot in front of another when I'll be delighted to come here and totter round it. Once started, directions are hardly necessary, but a few pointers may be helpful.

As the road descends from Newlands Hause towards Buttermere, it rounds a bend and a fine view of the dark fellside of Red Pike opposite is revealed, with the foaming cataracts of Sourmilk Gill pouring down into the mere. I've often thought of pausing here but the road is too narrow even to park my motor-bike, which I sometimes use in the Lakes in order to park in places that a car cannot use. (My dogs sometimes get left behind on these trips because Freddie has a tendency to jump out of the box on the back without my knowing he's gone, which is a bit inconvenient.)

Reaching the hamlet, swing right past the solid little parish church, then left into the ample parking area beside The Fish and The Bridge hotels (grid ref. 174169) – good for tea and scones later.

Now take the wide track, signposted to Buttermere and Scale Force, keep left at the fork, with Sourmilk Gill directly ahead, and trend towards the lakeside. The view towards the head of the lake is already dominated by the sharp upthrust edge of Fleetwith Pike, while the craggy skyline of Haystacks is visible

View across Buttermere to Mellbreak

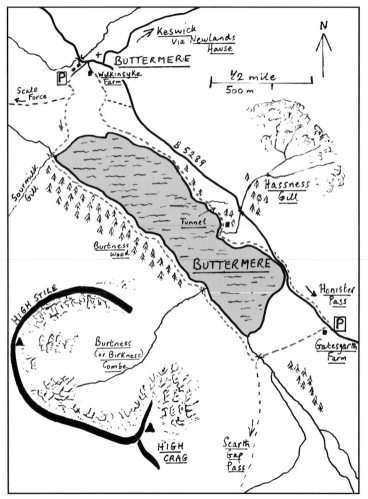

but soon disappears behind the intervening hillside as the track leads to the footbridge over the stream linking Buttermere to Crummock Water. Ignore the signs for Red Pike, cross the foot of Sourmilk Gill (splendid scrambling up the wide slabs on the way to the heights up here), and continue along the lakeside track through several gates and with Burtness Wood and steep fells on your right.

Across the lake, the rocky gullies funnelling into Hassness Gill (Hassnesshow Beck on OS map but never known as that) seam the fellside below Robinson and are well seen from here (more good scrambling for the enthusiast), particularly if you stay on the newer, permissive lakeside path rather than the older bridleway, which takes a higher line above Burtness Wood and restricts the prospect accordingly. Approaching the southern end of the lake the path to Scarth Gap is joined; turn the corner across Warnscale Beck and follow the track across the green and flat fields of Warnscale Bottom, backed by the heights of Green Crag and Haystacks, to Gatesgarth Farm. Here the tarmac road is the only way for a couple of hundred yards – and care is needed because of the traffic coming over Honister Pass – but as soon as the open lakeshore is reached, there is a signposted path around the little bay. From here are classic views across to Haystacks with a foreground of the well-known and very fine Buttermere pine trees.

The path stays close to the rocky eastern shore now, just above the water-line and with only a glimpse of the great white house of Hassness, one of

High Crag and Birkness Castle seen across Buttermere

whose owners, a certain George Benson, kept his men employed in the winter by excavating a short tunnel through the rock which the path now uses. Beyond the tunnel are wide grassy meadows and a lakeside fringe of superb mature beech, sycamore and oak trees which form a most elegant and pleasant parkland.

As the end of the lake is reached, the path leads straight ahead over some rocky ground and past Wilkinsyke Farm and so back to the village. It's easy. It's short. It's popular. But it's still a marvellous round.

71

The head of Ullswater with Keldas and Birkhouse Moor in view

PART TWO

Walks in the North-East

16.   Bowscale Fell and Bannerdale Crags

Best Map: OS 1:50,000 1¼″ to 1 mile (2cm to 1km) Landranger Sheet 90 (Penrith & Keswick). (Not on 1:25,000)

Distance: 4½ to 5½ miles/7.2km to 8.8km, depending on variation chosen

Highest elevation reached: 2306ft/703m

Height gained: 1580ft/482m

Overall star rating: * *

General level of exertion required: Medium

Time for the round: 3–3½ hours

Terrain: Mostly easy walking over grassy fells, though the descent from Bannerdale Crags requires care on the slaty rocks. An alternative descent is suggested.

Wide open spaces and rolling grassy fells characterise this walk, but there is no lack of contrast either for a gentle initial climb leads to an airy traverse around a fine cirque, an exhilarating descent and a return along the River Glenderamackin. Most of the walk would be fairly tedious in hill mist but this circuit is ideal for a day of fine weather when you feel like avoiding the crowds.

Almost midway between Keswick and Penrith, a secondary road goes off the A66 to Caldbeck and the attractive village of Mungrisdale is reached in a mile and a half. Just before you enter the village there is a clear view of the rocky end of Raven Crags straight ahead, well covered in gorse bushes, and this is the start of the walk. There is car parking on the roadside opposite the Mill Inn but it is more convenient to go further through the village, past the track signed to Mungrisdale Common (which is for the return) and past the little church. More parking places may usually be found when a fork in the road is reached, signposted for Hutton Roof (grid ref. 357323).

Immediately opposite this junction, a track leads to the right of a couple of houses. Follow this through a gate beside a little quarry and then turn immediately right up the end of the fell. A sketchy path slants up between the rocky outcrops and the gorse bushes and soon leads onto the broad whaleback of Bowscale Fell. This is uphill but easy walking, for a time through masses of bilberry, and as height is gained the whole walk becomes apparent. Bannerdale Crags become visible over the spur of The Tongue which largely obscured them from the valley, while Foule Crag and Sharp Edge on Blencathra are seen distantly.

Looking along the cirque of Bannerdale Crags; Bowscale Fell is on the right skyline

75

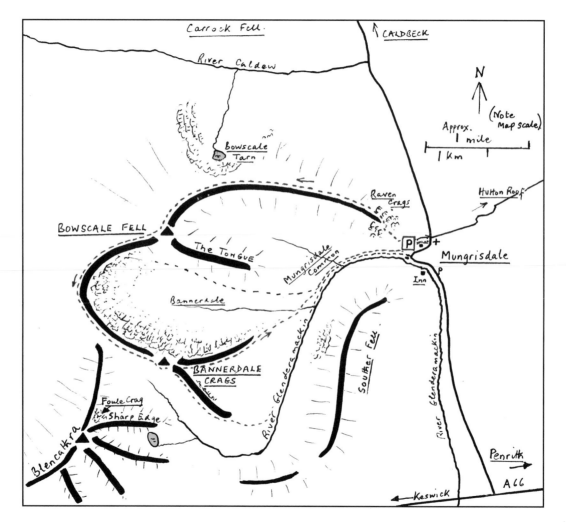

Press on towards the cairn on the skyline, but do peep over to the right just before reaching the highest point for a glimpse of Bowscale Tarn, a black pool which is visible from here although hidden from below. The access road to the mine on Carrock Fell and the buildings at the end of the road, also visible from here, are less attractive but fortunately a good distance away to the north. (The road from the mine spoils a potentially good walk over Carrock Fell, which is why it is not included in this book.)

From the cairn the way descends a little to cross a depression with a few stagnant pools in the peat, then swings round towards the cirque of Bannerdale Crags. The rocks are Skiddaw slate and well shattered but the views down Mungrisdale are worth the effort made to get here. A final pull leads up to the cairn on the highest point and an airy perch before the descent. From here a long spur projects eastwards, separating the rocky rim around which you have just walked from more, though less impressive crags further right, and this spur provides the way down. It starts on grass, rapidly leads to steeper and more shaly ground on the edge of the crags and care is needed in stepping down a couple of slate ledges. Easier terrain is soon reached and then an elegant grassy rib leads to the confluence of the Glenderamackin and the smaller beck issuing from Bannerdale. Here the path is joined leading north-eastwards along the river bank and so easily back to Mungrisdale village.

If the descent from Bannerdale Crags looks a bit too intimidating, a longer but easier way down can be found: instead of descending the spur, continue along the line of crags in a south-easterly direction until grassy slopes lead down to the Glenderamackin and the good path back to Mungrisdale.

Bannerdale Crags

17.   Artle Crag and Gatescarth

Best Map: OS 1:25,000 N.E. Sheet (Ullswater and
    Haweswater)

Distance: 4½ miles/7.2 km approx.

Highest elevation reached: 2333ft/711m

Height gained: 1600ft.488m

Overall star rating: */**

General level of exertion required: Fairly high

Time for the round: About 3 hours

Terrain: A mixture of paths; rolling, grassy,
    trackless fell; and bridleway. Reasonable
    visibility essential.

The head of Haweswater is for me a place charged with atmosphere; a combination of grandeur and great beauty, yet tinged with melancholy. I never saw the drowned village of Mardale Green, for the reservoir was created in the year of my birth, 1936, but – rather like Glencoe – I cannot help but be aware of its story. I have written in *On High Lakeland Fells* about the very fine circuit of Riggindale Crag, High Street and Harter Fell, but felt that I had to find a worthwhile walk that would enable a fellwalker with less time or ambition to see this fine cirque at its best – by looking into it. The fellside between Selside and Artle Crag is really the only possibility. The walk can be done in either direction and there is perhaps more in favour of doing it the opposite way to the one I describe here because of the easier climb up the pass than up rough fellside – but then you must contain your impatience for the views, which I can never do.

I prefer to park, not in the car park at the end of the Haweswater road, but at the point where there is some space beside it, where the 'Old Corpse Road', whose lowest section to the drowned village is cut in two by the new road, leads over to Swindale from the foot of Hopgill (grid ref. 479118). It is then a steady climb up the old bridleway from the gate at the roadside up the steep curves, on the left side of Hopgill Beck, reaching first one ruined building and then another a little higher, where the bearers perhaps rested before carrying their corpse on to Swindale and then to Shap for burial. The views from up here into the great cirque of fells around the head of the reservoir are really marvellous.

Now continue a little further up the corpse road, reach some white-topped marker posts and head over

The head of Haweswater from the Old Corpse Road

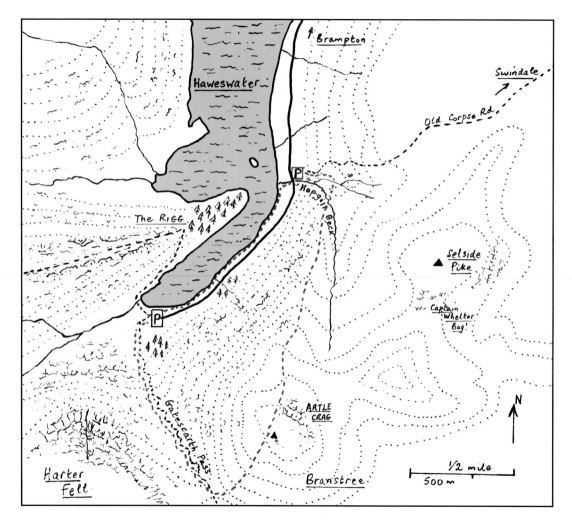

and up the moor to reach the cairn on Selside Pike, before following the broad line of the ridge southwards over the delights of Captain Whelter Bog to reach Artlecrag Pike. Or, choosing an easier line, you may use a little sheep-track that crosses the head of Hopgill at its first feasible place above the various small cascades and then points straight at a grassy spur heading directly for what looks like the top of Artle Crag. It isn't, of course. The top, as always, is a little further back, but you'll have some good exercise climbing this grassy fellside to reach it. On a visit with my family, who remember the climb well (and won't do it again for a long time!), we had the fine sight of a small herd of deer on the distant skyline just here. A marvellous sight.

When you reach the cairn on the top, you will see the seamed and craggy face of Harter Fell opposite and, five hundred feet below, the ribbon of the Gatescarth Pass track winding down to the valley again. There are no problems going down to it for it is just a grassy and stony slope. The way down the pass itself is perfectly straightforward, with a series of bends that are tight enough not to be an invitation to cut across them. They must have been good going for a packhorse.

But I was most impressed when my father-in-law, George Dracup, told me the tale of how he and five pals half-drove and half-manhandled a Morris Minor car up this very track over fifty years ago on the way to Longsleddale. He recalls staying the night in the Dun Bull in Mardale Green the night before, just a couple

Looking north-west across Haweswater

of years before it vanished beneath the rising waters for ever.

Reaching the valley again you may of course walk back along the road to the car, but it's much pleasanter to use the lakeside path.

81

18.   Place Fell

Best Map: OS 1:25,000 N.E. Sheet (Ullswater and
    Haweswater)

Distance: 3 miles/4.8km approx.

Highest elevation reached: 2154ft/657m

Height gained: 1650ft/503m

Overall star rating: * *

General level of exertion required: Medium/high

Time for the round: 3 hours

Terrain: Generally easy walking on good paths and
    tracks for the descent – which is the usual way
    up. The proposed way of ascent is, however, a
    bit tougher, up a natural rake line, involving
    grass, scree, boulders, not much of a path –
    and much more of an adventure.

Descending the Kirkstone Pass towards Ullswater, Place Fell is clearly seen beyond Brothers Water, framed by the slopes of Red Screes and those below Raven Edge, but it is much more complex than appears from this viewpoint and gives some excellent fellwalking.

The most popular way up Place Fell is from Patterdale by way of the slanting track from Side Farm up to Boardale Hause and then steeply up the shoulder of the fell. In indifferent weather, this is probably still the best way because the route is now so eroded and obvious that it would be fairly hard to lose it. I did originally intend to describe a walk over Place Fell which goes this way, descends to near Sandwick Bay and returns by way of Boardale, but felt that more adventurous walkers might like to see something of the more dramatic and secret side of Place Fell. The ascent I recommend is a little more strenuous, much more interesting, gives much better views over Ullswater and is a natural circular route. It is not on an obvious ridge and not easily apparent from below, though looking across Ullswater from Glenridding to the west flank, several possible lines can be seen slanting towards a shoulder of Birk Fell, which is part of the main massif. One of these uses a stream and does have a very sketchy path up (or, I suppose, mostly down) it. Another is further right and is the one to which I now refer.

There is plenty of parking at Patterdale (grid ref. 397157); then cross the valley floor either by Goldrill Bridge or by the track near the school and beside the George Starkey Hut to Side Farm. Pass between the whitewashed buildings and turn left down the bridle-

Place Fell seen from Brotherswater

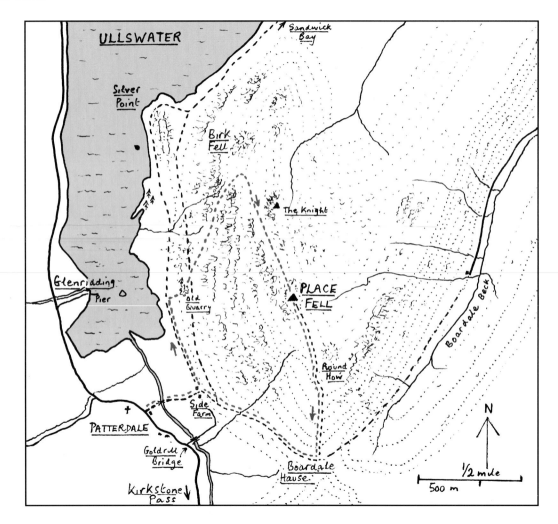

way for about a quarter of a mile alongside the wall. Just after passing a mighty and solitary oak, directly opposite the large ladder-stile (which leads over the wall into the camp-site), and before reaching a slate-built barn, turn right up the fellside through the bracken. Pass to the right of some spoil-heaps and an abandoned quarry hidden by ash trees then slant to the left across the fellside and follow the easier ground just above a rock outcrop.

Cross the well-used higher-level lakeside path and continue in the same diagonal direction below a great scree slope, above which is a belt of junipers. This natural line is interrupted occasionally by substantial scree, but don't be deflected for it gets easier as you climb steadily towards an obvious grassy shoulder, with junipers below and rockier ground above. The dark junipers can provide cover for the deer which roam the quieter parts of these fells and on the occasion when I first discovered this line I found, to my delight, that I was actually following two deer up it. The views over Ullswater are magnificent from here, high above the lake, but not obscured by the curve of the land, as is the case higher up. Continue in the same direction beyond the grassy shoulder, but now at an easier angle, towards another shoulder and then up a grassy runnel to find a cairn on a slight path. Swing sharply right now and follow a more distinct path south-eastwards, towards rock outcrops on the highest land, with another cairn ahead as your objective. A little further on, the OS triangulation point is reached, and you leave the wild country behind.

The descent is straightforward, on what is now an obvious path, south towards Round How and another cairn and then steeply down towards Boardale Hause. The final stage is the obvious track which slants to the right down the fellside back to Side Farm.

The summit of Place Fell, looking up to High Street

19.   Ullswater Lakeshore

Best Map: OS 1:25,000 N.E Sheet (Ullswater and Haweswater)

Distance: 6½ miles/10.4km

Highest elevation reached: 800ft/244m

Height gained: 325ft/99m

Overall star rating: * */ * * *

General level of exertion required: Low

Time for the round: About 4 hours, including the boat trip

Terrain: Easy going on good paths, occasionally muddy.

Ullswater has frequently been described as the most beautiful of the lakes and few will disagree. A walk along its southern shore can be delightful – but walking back the same way could be rather trying. By using the lake-steamer from Glenridding as far as Howtown, the day can be turned into a very good round trip. Obviously it is as well to check the sailing times and frequencies (usually about three times a day in summer), but once landed at Howtown the return walk takes two and a half to three hours at a gentle pace. It is an excellent family day out.

There is plenty of parking by the pier at Glenridding (grid ref. 390169); then book the single journey to Howtown, the first stop. The sail will give you a good idea of the way back on foot as you progress down the lake and the path is frequently visible along the fellside, except where it is obscured amongst the lovely woods, the juniper and the birch trees.

Leaving the jetty at Howtown, the path goes over a footbridge, along the shore, then up some steps to a higher-level terrace (with signs for Patterdale and Sandwick pointing the way all the time). The way curves under the slopes of Hallin Fell past the outcrop of Geordie's Crag and enters Hallinhag Wood where any youngsters in the party can enjoy a scramble on the rock of Kailpot Crag just inside the wood. Beyond the wood, the path leads via gates across the open fields of Sandwick to cross the Sandwick Beck, leaves the bay by going up the metalled road for a very short way and taking the Patterdale-signed path. This now undulates alongside a wall, crosses a footbridge over Scalehow Beck flowing down from the heights of Place Fell and then contours around the promontory. It has been interesting so far, but now the views really unfold as the Helvellyn massif comes into sight. The softer outlines of the fells at the northern end of the

Ullswater: the day's last ferry returns past Silver Point

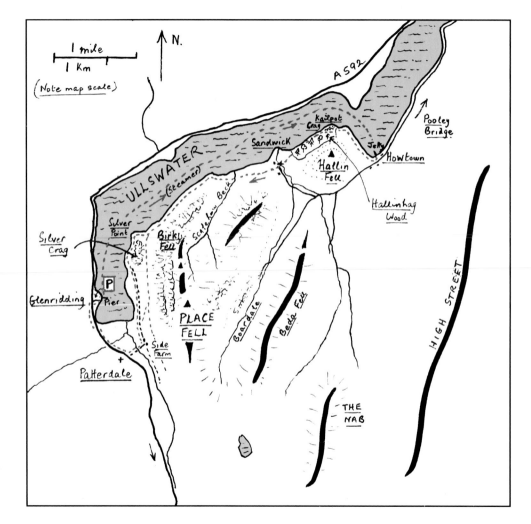

lake are left behind as the much more dramatic peaks appear ahead and a steady climb now leading to slightly higher ground allows the first of several fine prospects, made more so by the birch woods on the lower slopes of Birk Fell and the dark juniper on the higher ones.

The juniper woods on these slopes are very extensive and must certainly be the most abundant in Lakeland. When a thousand-foot-thick glacier was grinding down this valley ten thousand years ago it must have been 'real brass-monkey weather' and it isn't difficult to appreciate that only the toughest and hardiest little trees stood any chance of growth and regeneration in the hostile climate as the ice slowly retreated. But they obviously took a good hold here and have clung on ever since to this steep and craggy slope.

A little further ahead and the lake makes a sharp turn south at Silver Point where the juniper-covered and rocky hump of Silver Crag juts into the water. On reaching this, you may continue by the lakeshore past the Devil's Chimney (which is simply a tree-choked cleft – not much of a devil here) or take the more direct line which climbs to a higher level and stays up there. I prefer the higher path, for you can then more easily climb the little extra distance to the top of Silver Crag for a good view back along your walk and, if you descend the slopes a little through the tough juniper, for a most beautiful view to the head of Ullswater: the sort of view which really justifies its reputation.

It you stay on the higher path you should leave it a little way beyond the clump of trees round an old quarry to reach the main bridleway going to Side Farm – which the lower reaches anyway – then turn right across the valley bottom to Patterdale. A little tarmac-bashing is inevitable now, but after a short while, there is a path on the left of the road which is much pleasanter and leads quickly back to the field near the pier and a lakeside path to the car park.

The last stretch of the walk beside Ullswater

20. Beda Fell and The Nab

Best Map: OS 1:25,000 N.E. Sheet (Ullswater and Haweswater)

Distance: 7½ miles/12km approx.

Highest elevation reached: 2278ft/694m

Height gained: 1600ft/488m

Overall star rating: */* *

General level of exertion required: Medium

Time for the round: 3½–4 hours

Terrain: Mostly easy going on grass with fair paths, but good map-reading ability important in uncertain weather conditions.

The Martindale Fells are for connoisseurs of more secluded places, and are well worth the extra effort which is needed to approach them along the eastern side of Ullswater. They have harboured small herds of deer for many years, so leave your orange cagoule behind, wear sombre-coloured clothing and keep your gossiping low-key: you may be lucky and see some. This walk covers the Bannerdale skyline and although a little longer than many in this book the easy going makes it feel less.

The best parking is on the roadside near Garth Heads Farm at grid ref. 427186 (just up Boardale, reached via Pooley Bridge and Howtown) opposite a newish barn. Just beyond the barn and the first stone building on the left, a grass way between walls leads over a stile, signed for Martindale. This path climbs quickly to the ridge leading to Beda Fell (and is also the return route from Winter Crag Farm). From here there is a narrow but good path along the main line of the ridge, over a number of attractive little rocky outcrops, before a longer pull leads up to a rock 'beacon' which forms the first summit. A little further on is the prominent cairn on Beda Head.

From here, most of the rest of the walk is visible, going round the rim of Bannerdale, anti-clockwise, to the highest point on Rest Dodd and then out to the prominent spur of The Nab. Stride out for a way and then cross the path linking Boardale Hause with Bannerdale at Bedafell Knott, trending south on a reasonable path past a large cairn (which is the more noticeable because cairns are few and far between on these fells) heading for the higher ground ahead. A good view of Angle Tarn is soon seen below and the rocky ground to the right harbours the two Angletarn Pikes. It is always worth a little detour to scramble to their summits.

The track now descends towards the tarn and

Buck Crag and Rest Dodd seen from near the Angletarn Pikes

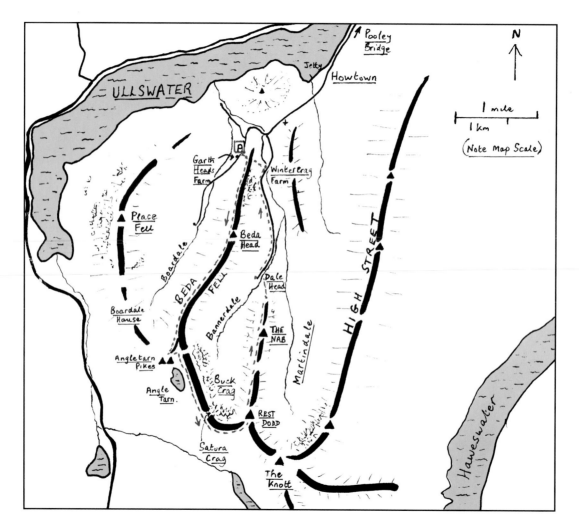

shortly joins the main path skirting its edge. Stay on the main path heading south-east and just below the Buck Crag–Satura Crag ridge, through a gate in a wall-corner to a peaty hause; this can be a wonderful vantage point for views down Bannerdale. Beyond here the path descends a little and starts to swing right in order to cross a wall on the way to The Knott and High Street, but the grassy slopes of Rest Dodd rise steadily and more steeply to the left, offering a new challenge. That's where the top is, so leave the main path and climb up alongside the wall to the summit. This is your highest point and you'll probably be glad to turn the achievement of reaching it into an excuse for a little rest.

From here descend directly northwards to a gap in the wall and then across a depression of peat-hags before a gentle pull up to the summit of The Nab. Don't take the stalker's path which avoids the top and steers leftwards round the shoulder.

This is certainly an area in which to linger, to lie quietly and inconspicuously on the fellside and just watch and listen for a while. You may see nothing more exciting than sheep and the odd black raven or buzzard circling the sky. But you might hear the roaring of stags – a thrilling sound – and watch small herds of deer move away around the curve of the fell as they catch your scent.

Descend The Nab directly to a gap in the wall below Nab End and then down the grassy slopes to a footbridge across Bannerdale Beck, just outside Dale Head Farm. From here there is a good track down

Bannerdale to reach Winter Crag Farm, then a last little climb back up Howstead Brow on the path leading over the toe of the Beda Fell ridge to the walled lane and so to your starting point.

Looking down Bannerdale: Beda Fell is on the left, The Nab on the right

21. Sheffield Pike

Sheffield Pike is a fine viewpoint, particularly of the Helvellyn Group and of the length of Ullswater and is itself probably best seen from the southern shore of the lake where it rises steeply above Glenridding. This walk uses the Ullswater side of the Sticks Pass for the ascent, but a steeper and more exciting way down from the tops to give a good round.

Glencoynedale is about a mile north of Glenridding and there is car parking in several places on the landward side of the main road, particularly at Glencoyne Bridge (grid ref. 387188) and also at the main road end of the track leading to the little hamlet (signed by a finger-post) of Seldom Seen. Thereafter, all the tracks or paths going west, whether skirting Glencoyne Wood or past the farmstead, lead to the well-hidden hamlet at Seldom Seen and so on to Sticks Pass. The way climbs steadily, initially alongside a wall, though with diversions around fallen storm-blown trees which block the path in places. After about 500ft of height has been gained, the path leads onto open fellside and continues upwards, towards the broad and peaty hause at the left-hand side of the head of the dale. As this is gained (the main path continuing towards Sticks Pass) a slighter path leads off left and then curves back eastwards along the broad ridge of Sheffield Pike itself. It is now only a short distance to the beacon, a pile of rocks on the summit amongst which will be found a curious stone with the characters H M E R 1830 chiselled into it, presumably the initials of an early visitor to the Pike. A little lower down is a windbreak shelter from which, in more comfort, the play of light and shade on the surrounding hills may be enjoyed.

Sheffield Pike seen across Ullswater

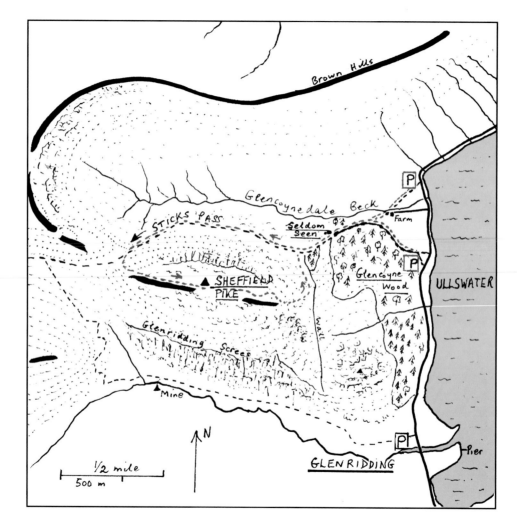

Brown Hills

Glencoynedale Beck

STICKS PASS

Seldom
Seen

Farm

Glencoyne
Wood

ULLSWATER

▲ SHEFFIELD
PIKE

Wall

Glenridding Screes

▲ Mine

GLENRIDDING

Pier

↑ N

½ mile
500 m

View from Sheffield Pike over Birkhouse Moor to Fairfield on the skyline

To descend, if you have come up in your wellies or your trendy canvas footwear, you had better reverse the ascent route in its entirety. If you are properly shod walk west, towards the bulk of Place Fell seen across Ullswater, following the line pointed out by about four cairns. Thereafter, there are only sketchy sheep tracks, or no tracks, to help you along, but heathery fell leads down a very broad and open gully towards Ullswater, aiming for a bare rocky top with conifers clothing its flank and a wall that runs right across and over the fell. Turn down left beside the wall outside the plantation and the Sticks Pass footpath is soon rejoined. It is now only a short descent back to the starting-point.

22.   Satura Crag and Angletarn Pikes

Best Map: OS 1:25,000 N.E. Sheet (Ullswater and Haweswater)

Distance: 5 miles/8km

Highest elevation reached: 1800ft/549m

Height gained: 1300ft/396m

Overall star rating: * *

General level of exertion required: Medium/high

Time for the round: 3 hours

Terrain: Good paths over most of the distance, though they aren't quite so obvious on the proposed approach to Satura Crag. This is a good walk even in mediocre weather, so long as you can see the way up.

Angle Tarn itelf is an attractive sheet of water high on the fellside at the foot of the two pikes, which stand out clearly as rocky high-points, well seen from various places on the north side of the Kirkstone Pass. This walk traverses them from that direction by way of Satura Crag.

Start from the car park at grid ref. 410130 on the far side of Hartsop village but, as I always do when there is a chance to avoid the most popular way, instead of rushing off with everybody else up the main track east towards Hayeswater Gill (which is admittedly a perfectly feasible but longer and much less interesting way than that here proposed), walk back towards the main road. In twenty paces or so a discreet footpath sign points right up a lane between cottages. This swings left uphill through a gate and in a further twenty paces a green lane leads sharply and horizontally back right. (The track that you have just left leads towards Ullswater and will be used on the return).

Follow this green lane outside the wall in the general direction of Hayeswater Gill (south-east), through a gate and then between walls, until the way is barred by another wall and you find yourself in the bottom corner of a large field. With due consideration for the sheep who will be munching there, walk up beside the wall, through another gate and then, following a stream runnel, join a natural, slanting, grassy rake leading steadily upwards.

By the time this rake starts to peter out, you are well up the fellside and the reservoir of Hayeswater should be in view to the right, below Gray Crag on its west side. Continue directly in the same line towards knobbly rocks on the skyline, cross an old wire fence

View from Satura Crag to High Street, Hayeswater and Gray Crag

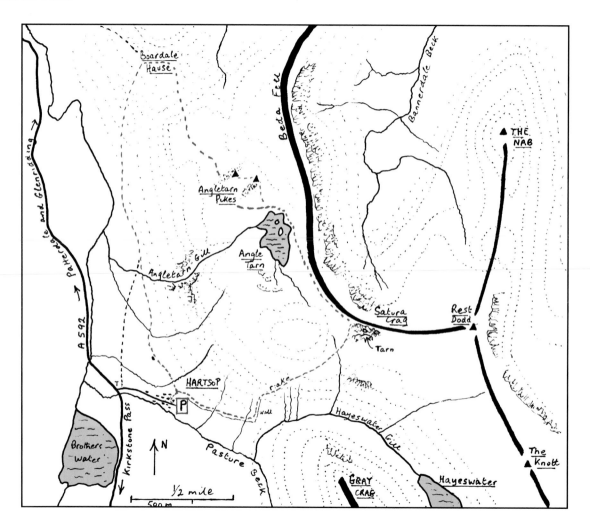

Boardale
Hause

Bannerdale Beck

Beda Fell

Patterdale and Glenridding

A 592

THE
NAB

Angletarn
Pikes

Angletarn Gill

Angle
Tarn

Satura
Crag

Rest
Dodd

Tarn

HARTSOP

Rake

wall

Hayeswater Gill

Kirkstone Pass

Brothers
Water

N

Pasture Beck

GRAY
CRAG

Hayeswater

The
Knott

½ mile

500 m

which long ago gave up keeping anything in or out, and finally scramble up some steep grass. The rocks prove to be the Hartsop side of Satura Crag, which is much more of a crag on the Bannerdale side. A tiny little L-shaped tarn is trapped amongst them, and the spot provides a dramatic perch for the views to High Street, Hayeswater and Gray Crag in particular.

A few paces away is the normal path and a short walk north-westwards along it brings Angle Tarn into view, with a distant prospect of the fells around Helvellyn. The path skirts the tarn, but nobody who enjoyed the sporting way up to Satura Crag can surely resist the chance now to scramble to the summits above it, the Angletarn Pikes themselves. The views are good, but it's the scrambling up there that makes them better still before you have to return to the path. This is well-worn now (in fact there is both a lower and a higher path, but they join up further on) and leads easily to the meeting of ways on Boardale Hause. You won't find the 'Chapel in the Hause' which is marked on the map, though you may find a few scattered and no doubt consecrated stones. Here swing to the left beside the beck, then cross it and follow the obvious path down an alternately stony and grassy track, taking a slanting diagonal line beside the buried (but detectable) water conduit towards Brotherswater.

At the foot of Angletarn Gill, rather than taking the footbridge leading to the lower-level lane returning to Hartsop, cross the footbridge but then go along the wall for thirty paces until a stone stile leads across

it to a much more interesting footpath. This leads past the beautifully situated house called 'Grey Rigg' and then goes directly to the upper part of Hartsop village and the car park.

Angle Tarn from near one of its Pikes, looking south

101

23.   Gowbarrow Fell

Best Map: OS 1:25,000 N.E. Sheet (Ullswater and Haweswater)

Distance: 3½ miles/5.6km approx.

Highest elevation reached: 1578ft/481m

Height gained: 1100ft/335m

Overall star rating: **/***

General level of exertion required: Fairly low

Time for the round: 2–3 hours

Terrain: Mostly on good paths over grassy fellside but with the odd rougher and boggier patch. There should be few problems in less than perfect weather.

To wander over Gowbarrow Fell, with its wonderful views over Ullswater, then to return via the spectacular cascade of Aira Force (avoiding nearly all the 'tourist-zone' down near the lakeside) is a delightful experience and this walk describes such a possibility.

The A5091 links the A66 Penrith–Keswick road with that along the north shore of Ullswater (the A592), passing through the village of Dockray. This road climbs towards Dockray from the lakeside and just before reaching the village, there is a quarry on the left and a large lay-by on the right-hand side with the sign 'National Trust Gowbarrow', which is a good place to park (grid ref. 396212). The sign also supposedly restricts your length of stay here – a bit of bureaucracy that is rightly ignored by all who don't intend to be rushed over their enjoyment of such a fine walk as this. Perhaps it's intended to restrict you from having a picnic by the river bank? A footpath leads down the fields from here to Aira Beck and this is crossed by means of a 'strid' over the limestone blocks through which the water rushes at its narrowest point. You can quite literally stand with one foot on one side and one on the other here but if your nerves won't stand this, you can go downstream for a couple of hundred paces to find a footbridge and then go back up the other bank. (Don't waste your time going upstream before crossing because the way is barred). If you park in Dockray itself after the road has crossed the beck, there is a path along the other bank. Personally I prefer the little excitement of the strid.

Now go upstream on the east bank for a hundred paces and then follow various paths and sheep tracks slanting uphill and leftwards to the north-east, wandering up through the bracken, to reach the trig point

Walkers on Green Hill; looking across Ullswater to Hallin Fell and the Martindale Fells

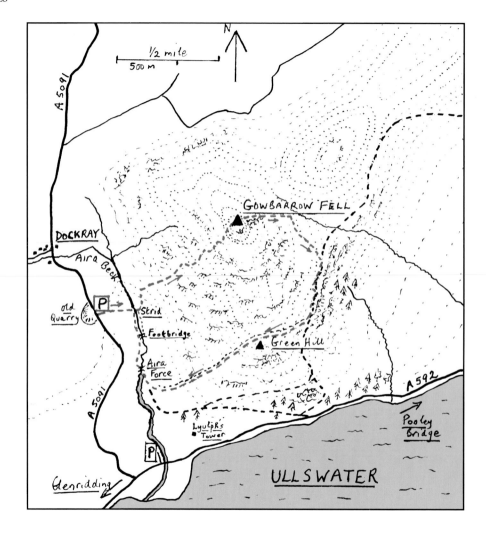

on the summit. There are no worthwhile views from here, for a brackeny moor blocks the prospect over Ullswater, but descend a little spur from the summit towards a stile in a corner where two walls meet and this leads to a little beck tinkling towards Ullswater. Swing sharply right before meeting the stream and cross rougher ground for a little way before descending gently to intersect with a good path which now contours the side of the fell above Ullswater. This is a delightful path, virtually level for much of the way, skirting just above little crags and woods and heading generally towards the lake.

When a choice of ways arrives, take the right fork, which quickly leads up to the superb viewpoint of Green Hill, a little eminence on the fellside which gives lovely views along the lake and particularly towards its head. We stood here once when the sky turned almost black overhead and it looked as if a mighty downpour was about to start. But then a shaft of sunlight struck down through the clouds and illuminated, spotlit, an area of Patterdale. Slowly it travelled up the fellside towards the higher peaks and then disappeared. Then within five minutes the clouds rolled back and the risk of a cloudburst passed.

From here a good path now slants gently downhill across the fell towards Aira Beck, passing above the battlements and turrets of Lyulph's Tower, and join- ing the main path to Aira Force just before reaching the footbridge which spans the cascade at its top. It's almost always worth making the short descent to the viewpoint below the falls because they are most

Aira Force

spectacular seen from there, then circling up the other side (on a good path) back to the bridge. Now leave the tourists rushing back to their coaches and teas and wander back upstream on a good path, but on the left-hand side of the Aira Beck, to reach another but much shorter cascade. Just above it is the strid again and the footpath back over the fields to the car.

105

24. Hallin Fell

Best Map: OS 1:25,000 N.E. Sheet (Ullswater and Haweswater)

Distance: 2 miles/3.2km approx. (plus steamer journey)

Highest elevation reached: 1271ft/387m

Height gained: 770ft/235m

Overall star rating: * *

General level of exertion required: Medium

Time for the round: 4 hours, including the boat trip.

Terrain: Generally easy going on good paths or grassy slopes. The low altitude of the fell means that it is often well below the prevailing cloud ceiling.

Hallin Fell projects boldly into Ullswater on its south-eastern shore. It's only a little tiddler, but it's quite isolated from the surrounding fells, a splendid viewpoint and the more noticeable for having a tall stone obelisk, visible for miles, on its summit. The ascent can be made in a twenty-minute burst of energy, or it can be treated as a really enjoyable walk in its own right, very suitable for a family walk (however you define it), a short day, or even a long one if you stop often enough. I prefer wild country to the other sort and so this walk deliberately chooses a natural line to the top.

For most people coming from the other side of Ullswater, reaching Howtown from Patterdale via Pooley Bridge is a time-consuming hassle, unless you take the lake steamer starting from the pier at Glenridding. There is ample parking there (grid ref. 390169), the boat sails regularly, gives a scenic trip along the best part of Ullswater and makes its first stop at Howtown. Make sure you check the return times so there is ample opportunity to climb Hallin Fell and return the same way. (I may add that on a recent visit, by road, there had been so much rain that Ullswater was slopping over the tarmac and a boat would have been needed to reach the dry land even from the Howtown jetty, but these were exceptional circumstances.)

From the jetty at Howtown, follow the path over a footbridge and along the lake shore through a couple of wicket-gates, following signs for Patterdale and Sandwick all the time, up some steps and turn right onto a terrace well above the shoreline, alongside a wall. The path runs parallel to the lakeside, turns the

Hallin Fell seen across Ullswater

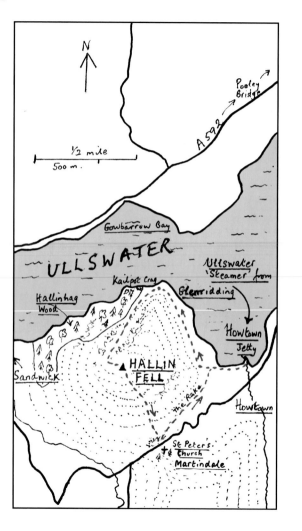

corner and approaches Kailpot Crag just inside Hall-inhag Wood. Immediately before entering the wood, an infrequently used path goes left, climbing steeply through the bracken and between two rock outcrops, one a little higher than the other. Above the higher rocks, the bracken is much less dense, the angle eases and a slanting, natural grassy rake leads upwards and across a fellside, just below the line of the ridge which is itself a little higher up. There is a path of sorts, used by sheep and a few other wanderers like yourself: nothing much, but enough.

Nearing a shoulder of the fell, the rake comes to an end and you must scramble very easily upwards to the fine obelisk on the summit. This is about twelve feet high and six feet broad at its base, built mostly of granite (or something like that – I'm no geologist) but with two blocks of a softer stone inset high up, one above the other, on the northern side. On the upper stone (amongst other carvings, mostly the scratchings of hooligans, are chiselled the initials IW. SP 19. On the lower one there is a large letter B and, more faintly, the date 1864. Perhaps to commemorate the builder? Whoever he was, he certainly built a solid monument on a fine viewpoint. Have a look at the Martindale fells from here: some splendid walking country.

The descent is easier and very straightforward. Go down the grassy slopes on any of several paths which are all close together, heading for the nearest building in sight, which is St Peter's Church, Martindale. This is situated on a hause, with a clump of sheltering

Looking north from Place Fell, with Hallin Fell in the middle distance

trees, where the road climbs in hairpin-bends round the back of Hallin Fell into Martindale. Cars are often parked here, opposite the church, while their owners take the soft option of climbing the fell with this little height advantage. Don't walk down the road, for a grass track called The Rake leads directly from the hause at a much more gentle angle back towards the Howtown jetty.

25. Gill Crag Ridge and Dovedale

Best Map: OS 1:25,000 N.E. Sheet (Ullswater and Haweswater)

Distance: 4 miles/6.4km approx.

Highest elevation reached: 1870ft/570m

Height gained: 1350ft/411m

Overall star rating: *

General level of exertion required: Medium

Time for round: 2½–3 hours

Terrain: A sketchy path to the ridge, a good one on it, a rougher descent, but then a good path down Dovedale. Because this is essentially a ridge walk, it gives few problems even in mist.

This walk is very simple in concept: climb up to and walk the ridge overlooking both Deepdale and Dovedale, with splendid views of the heads of both, then descend the beautiful Dovedale to return. It gives the best of the views without having to do either of the greater cirques of Dovedale or Deepdale.

There is a good car park at the northern end of Brothers Water (grid ref. 403134) just where the A592 crosses the Goldrill Beck and there is a useful and interesting National Park signboard about the particular problems of farming in Dovedale just beside the track which leads southwards along the west side of Brothers Water. Don't rush off along the track though, because immediately beyond the signboard a path, not always obvious, particularly in summer when the trees are in leaf, climbs steeply into Low Wood to the right of the main track. In a few yards, there is a stile and then another with a thoughtful little gate at its foot which can be lifted to let an animal through. I personally appreciate this because then I don't have to lift the muddy little bodies of my two Schnauzers. The path, rather sketchy in places, now climbs steadily towards the ridge above. As it gets above the tree line, you see a fine prospect of Brothers Water and many of the High Street fells, with the attractive village of Hartsop nestling below.

The path begins to peter out but then the line of an old collapsed wall is reached and this can be followed up the fellside to reach a cairn. Ahead is a very solid wall, running down the length of the main ridge. Don't attempt to cross this here; stay to the left of the wall on the sketchy path until you reach a stile, then cross over to the main line of the ridge. You will have fine views across Dovedale up to this point. The ridge is now broad and open until the rockier high ground

Looking up Dovedale from Brotherswater

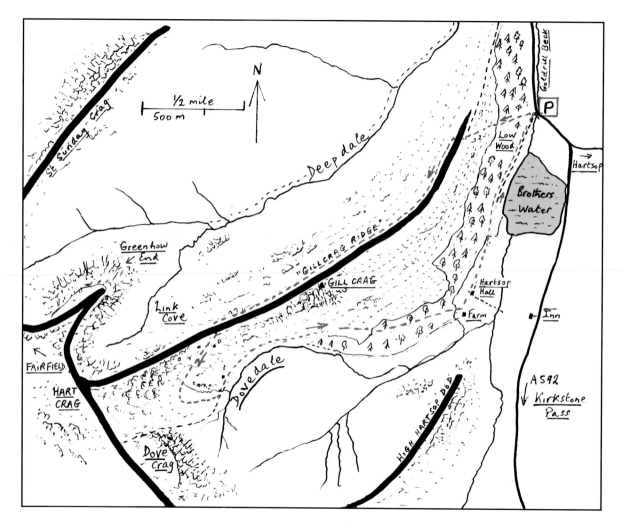

of Gill Crag is reached, and then there are increasingly good views of the magnificent wild head of Deepdale with Link Cove and Greenhow End on the right side and the impressive cliffs of Dove Crag – scene of many great rock-climbing epics – on the left. Beyond Gill Crag the ridge is broader again and, as you progress, the ground becomes more like a Derbyshire moor, with peat-hags and rocky outcrops and the path winding amongst them, before it begins a slow climb towards the heights of Hart Crag ahead.

Now leave the beaten track and veer to the left, slanting across the fell towards Dove Crag, choosing your own line but not losing height and, though you may be tempted, not descending the course of the beck which goes down rather too abruptly for comfort. Cross the beck to get nearer to Dove Crag and you will intersect with a path which will be found going down a normally dry and fairly shallow gully. This now leads fairly steeply downhill past a ruined building and becomes steadily better as it reaches more level ground.

The last stage of this walk down Dovedale is really a delightful one, downhill all the way to the valley floor, on a path which goes just above the beck and then wanders through ancient woods, with glimpses all the time of the greener pastures below and the sound of the tumbling waters always in your ears. Beyond the farm buildings, the way leads round to the back of Hartsop Hall and joins a level farm track which enables you to wander along the side of the beautiful Brothers Water and back to the car park.

The head of Deepdale from the Gill Crag ridge above Brotherswater

113

26. Gray Crag

Gray Crag is rather like a neglected central prong in a trident, ignored in favour of its eastern neighbour, High Street, but it is a shapely fell in its own right and usually peaceful when the crowds are tramping the old Roman roadway. On three occasions, I have seen a small herd of deer move quickly away up the slopes of Gray Crag as I drew close, but I have never seen them on High Street. I hear so often the cry that the Lake District is crowded, but there are lots of places to go that aren't – when you know where they are. This is one of them.

The start is at the very attractive village of Hartsop, just beyond Brothers Water on the north side of the Kirkstone Pass, and the car park is at grid ref. 410130 on the far side of the village. As you enter, the steep end of Gray Crag is very evident straight ahead. We are, however, going to steal up on it from behind and use that blunt nose as the way down. So, going through the car park gate, turn right immediately and follow the 'Pasture Beck' sign over the stream and then left up its right bank (true left, in the direction of flow) through sheep pastures, to the final intake wall, gate and stile. (The main path to Hayeswater Gill is seen on the other (left) side of the valley floor).

The path now stays close to the course of the beck, with the hause, col, or pass of Threshthwaite Mouth ahead as its obvious objective, though it is probably of more recent origin than the Roman way which used Hagg Gill on the far side and climbed more rapidly to the then more defensible and less afforested ridges. It passes below steep crags on the west side (Raven Crag, Threshthwaite Mouth) which have seen some

*Gray Crag from the
village of Hartsop*

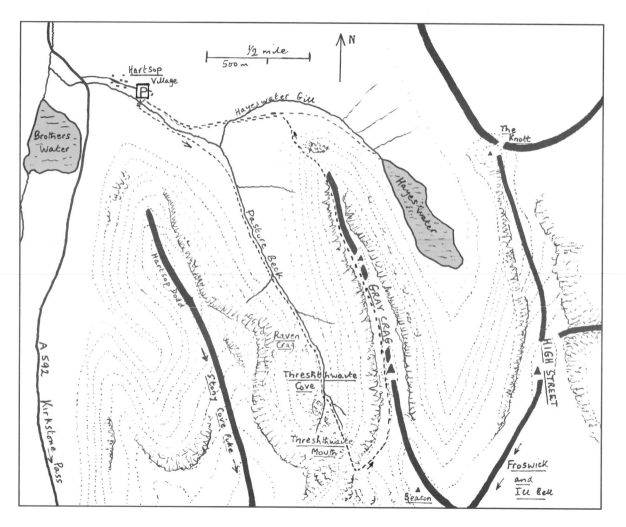

of the most recent rock-climbing developments in the area and then becomes less obvious as it wanders amongst rocks and stones on the last section.

Reaching the pass go left up scrabbly scree and rocks – the path is steep and loose here and crampons are often needed in winter – but as height is gained, veer to the left side of the tumbledown wall, cross the remains of another and head for the broad grassy ridge of Gray Crag itself. You will shortly be able to have your lunch in solitude, although if it's windy you will have to tuck yourself into a grough between peat-hags or hide in a grassy hollow, for it is exposed to the elements up here. You won't be troubled by the litter and orange peel around Threshthwaite Beacon just a little distance away and will be able to enjoy much the same views to High Street, down to Hayeswater and of course to Ullswater.

For the descent, continue northwards. The path along the summit ridge peters out as others before you have sought for the best line of descent and been undecided. I think it is best to go straight down initially, but there is an outcrop of steep rocks just a little way down the end of the fell and it's best to trend slightly to one side of the ridge to avoid them. If you go left, you can follow the line of a wall which goes part of the way down the fell and then, for no apparent reason, ends. It could hardly have been a shortage of stone. However, just beyond this is a corner of the intake-field wall, beside which is the main Hayeswater Gill track which leads back to the car park.

Looking up Pasture Beck to Threshthwaite Mouth, with Gray Crag on the left

Fell Foot Farm with Blake Rigg behind

PART THREE

Walks in the South-West

27. Black Combe

Best Map: OS 1:50,000 1¼" to 1 mile (2cm to 1km) Landranger Sheet 96 (Barrow-in-Furness). (Not on 1:25,000 scale maps.)

Distance: 3½ miles/5.6km approx.

Highest elevation reached: 1970ft/600m

Height gained: 1800ft/549km

Overall star rating: * *

General level of exertion required: Medium/high

Time for the round: 2½ – 3 hours

Terrain: Fairly easy walking over grassy fells, but a steepish descent. It is a rather featureless place to be in, in a mist, so best avoided in doubtful weather.

Situated right on the southern border of the Lake District National Park, the hills of Black Combe (and White Combe) just look like a long and sloping moor from the north but are seen to be much more interesting when viewed across the Duddon Estuary, from the winding coastal road that leads to Whitehaven and Workington in west Cumbria. They are a last major swelling upthrust on the long ridge from Bowfell south-westwards to the sea and this walk tours the cirque of crags that are their best and most dominant feature.

I made about four different visits to Black Combe trying to sort out the best way to go and the longest and weariest way is, as perhaps you won't be too surprised to learn by now, the public footpath shown on the map from near Whitbeck and returning to near Whicham. It's all right for a fell-runner or a lad on a mountain-bike, but there's no view – except out to sea – until you're at the top.

To make the most of Black Combe, park at Beckside just on the left of the main A595 road at grid ref. 152847 where there is space for a few cars. Now go up the lane opposite, which is obviously heading up the steep-sided valley between Black Combe and White Combe. Keep to the right of the cottages and up the grassy path on the right bank of the little stream, over a stile by a gate, through a last gate in the intake wall and straight up the gill. At the point where another stream comes in from the left (in fact, flowing from the cirque of Black Combe) you could well make this walk shorter by scrambling up the grassy ridge on its right bank, but it's at a fairly steep angle. I found it better to keep going up the main gill,

Black Combe from Foxfield, seen across the Duddon Estuary

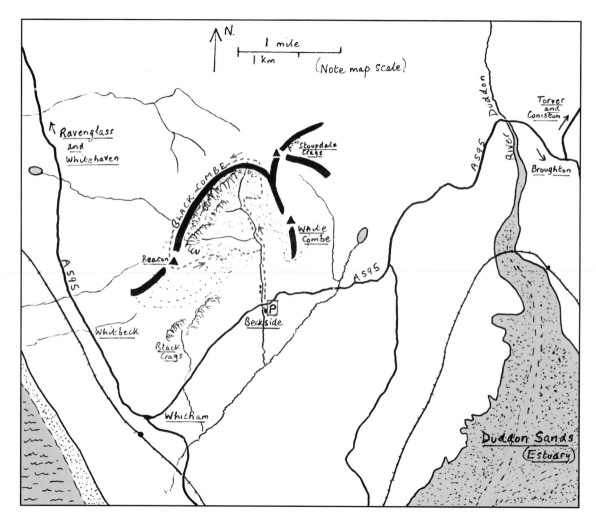

for you are encouraged by being able to see a dip in the ridge at the top. There isn't much of a path but then you are able to see and use a slanting rake where a long 'zig' goes out to the right, followed by a 'zag' back to the left to reach the hause itself. The cairn on the top of White Combe is about half a mile to the south-east and virtually on the same level as you are if you want to wander over there. From the hause, however, a sketchy path swings left (south) in a gentle but steady ascent over moorland for about a mile towards Black Combe. The most dramatic views are those down the cirque of shattered crags out over the Duddon Estuary and in fact these are much better than anything from the actual summit, for the cairn lies a way back on a flat moor. Descend a short way from the cairn, past a little tarn, to the south and there is a huge beacon from where there are views to Barrow, Millom and the Isle of Walney.

I was sitting there once having a sandwich, with my two dogs, Henry and Freddie, scrounging as usual, when I was approached by a chap whom I'd never met before. After chatting for a while, he hesitated and then said, "I think I ought to know those two dogs, shouldn't I?" (People always recognise the dogs, not me.) "When's your next book coming out?"

I've tried various ways of descent from the top. One route descended south towards Black Crags and then contoured back north-eastwards to reach Beckside but I got into a muddle with fences near the bottom. By far the best is to return to the cirque of crags and descend the long grassy spur that forms its southern arm (the left-hand end as you look into the cirque from a distance). You are quickly down that way and have no road-walking to do either.

View from the rim of Black Combe to the Duddon Estuary

28.   Muncaster Fell

Best Map: OS 1:25,000 S.W. Sheet (Wast Water
   and Coniston)

Distance: 5 miles/8km approx.

Highest elevation reached: 758ft/231m

Height gained: 700ft/213m

Overall star rating: */**

General level of exertion required: Medium/low

Time for the round: 4 hours – of which half the time
   is walking

Terrain: Reasonable tracks and paths, some of
   which can be boggy. The way is
   straightforward though and should give few
   problems in poor weather.

Muncaster Fell is the ridge at the western end of Eskdale which separates it from the land just south of Wasdale. Its crossing is a fine walk, preferably from south to north, because you then have the splendid Eskdale fells in sight most of the time. There is no obvious return way except back up the road, but, when combined with a journey on the Ravenglass &

Eskdale miniature railway as the other half of the round, the day becomes an excellent expedition, very suitable for an active family.

The train ride from either Eskdale Green station (grid ref. 145998) – or Irton Road station which is next along the line to Ravenglass – to Muncaster Mill is a delightful journey in the mini-carriages, puffing along below the steep fellside. In the spring, it is especially attractive with daffodils alongside the track and the sweet-scented gorse in flower. The train runs regularly throughout the season from end-March to end-October, with occasional winter days as well. If in doubt, telephone Ravenglass 226 for the latest information.

Alight at Muncaster Mill (grid ref. 095978), and be sure to spare some time to have a look at the restored and working water-powered corn mill. The miller is a real enthusiast and I learned a great deal about bread as a result. I was so impressed that I purchased a 14lb bag (6½kg) bag of organically grown stone-ground wholemeal flour, added it to my rucksack load and carried it for the rest of the journey.

Leaving the mill, go through the yard, turn right at the sign 'Bridleway Castle and Ravenglass' (not the 'Bridleway Eskdale' one) and then in twenty paces go sharp left uphill at another sign for the castle. The track climbs through bracken and joins a forest track

*'L'al Ratty' approaching
Eskdale Green Station*

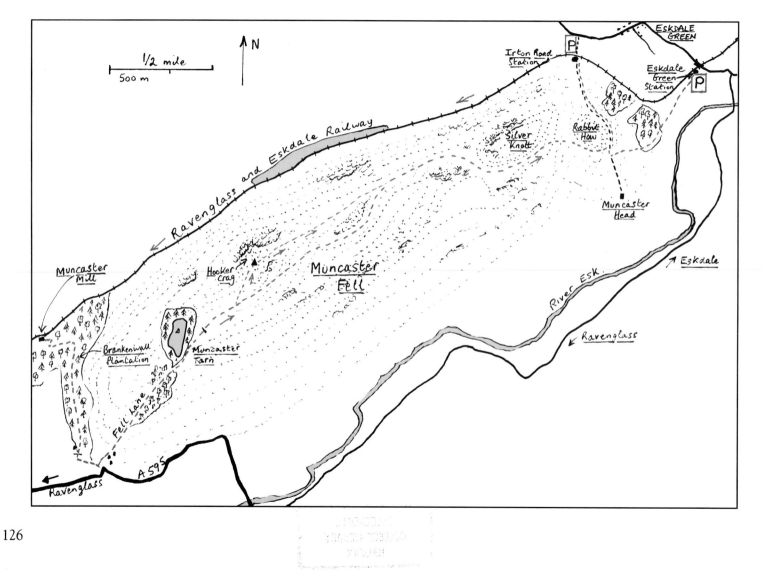

1/2 mile

500 m

N

ESKDALE
GREEN

Irton Road
Station

P

Eskdale
Green
Station

P

Ravenglass and Eskdale Railway

Silver
Knott

Rabbit
How

Muncaster
Head

Eskdale

River Esk

Muncaster
Mill

Hooker
Crag

Muncaster
Fell

Ravenglass

Brankenwall
Plantation

Muncaster
Tarn

Fell Lane

A 595

Ravenglass

going up a wide ravine (Brankenwall Plantation) where, in early summer, lovely flowering rhododendrons compensate for the slutch under your feet. At the end of the plantation, turn left through a gate, meet the Ravenglass–Bootle road in a few more yards and immediately turn left again at the sign 'Public Bridleway Eskdale and Hard Knott'. This is Fell Lane, a good and straight track between obviously ancient stone walls and perhaps used by the Romans on their way from Hardknott fort. It climbs steadily through more rhododendrons, birch and pine and has retrospective views to the shining sea and the nature reserve of the Ravenglass Dunes (the 'Gullery'). Muncaster Tarn is passed on the left, though it is largely hidden in the forestry, and then, beyond a gate, a beacon can be seen on the open fell at last.

Leave the track here and climb up to this highest point – Hooker Crag – where the beacon proves to be the OS triangulation point and from where there are fine views in all directions. Ahead, to the east, is Eskdale with its southern wall of intriguing knobbly tops and crags, and Harter Fell standing proud above them. To the south is the line of fells ending in Black Combe: to the north is Whin Rigg, the rocky fell-tops of Buckbarrow and the deep slash of Wasdale between them. To the west, even the great towers of the Sellafield nuclear power station, which dominate the shoreline, seem peaceful enough.

Return to the track if you choose, but now is your chance to wander freely for a while along the undulating high land, over the bracken- and heather-covered fell, choosing your own little path. You have to descend soon enough anyway to rejoin the track where it meets, and passes through, an old wall, but even here it is drier on the higher land.

Ahead rises Silver Knott, another rocky lump with a bog in the intervening depression, but the path swings right to avoid both bog and rocks, up a section of the way whose solid and well-assembled stone blocks suggest that it was at some time constructed for horse-and-carriage traffic. The last stage of the descent, with the village of Eskdale Green in view, is down to Rabbit How, which is well named; it is covered in gorse bushes and, in winter, is grazed by cows who churn the ground into quagmires. Some diversions from the path here may well be desirable to avoid getting mud up to your own fetlocks.

Reaching the valley bottom, the path meets a broad track. Turn left (north) here and follow it directly to the car park at Irton Road station. Or, if you started from Eskdale Green station (which is a little way from the village itself), turn right (south) for just a few paces on the track towards Muncaster Head and then turn left along a good path. This quickly leads to a leafy lane alongside the railway line, reaching the station a few moments later.

127

29. Buckbarrow

Best Map: OS 1:25,000 S.W. Sheet (Wast Water and Coniston)

Distance: 3½ miles/5.6km approx. for the shorter route, 6 miles/10km if you go to Seatallan

Highest elevation reached: 1443ft/440m (If you go up to Seatallan, 2770ft/693km)

Height gained: 1230ft/375m (2057ft/627m)

Overall star rating: *

General level of exertion required: Medium/high

Time for the round: About 2 hours; or 3½ hours if Seatallan is included

Terrain: A good path as far as Greendale Tarn, then roughish fellside.

Nearly everybody entering Wasdale with serious intent (from which I exclude those who simply park, sit in their cars and read their over-weighty newspapers) rushes up to the head of the valley to be amongst the splendid fells awaiting them up there. Consequently the fine crags of Buckbarrow at the southern end of the lake tend to be overlooked, especially since they are partly hidden and are over the left shoulder of any traveller entering Wasdale by any other than the Gosforth road. The actual fell-top, which is some way back from Buckbarrow itself, is called Glade How, but that is only a rock-pimple on a moor. To be on top of the real crags is something quite different. Even those keen fellwalkers and climbers who are regular visitors to Wasdale and know the views from the valley or from Yewbarrow, may find, as I certainly did, a new perspective from a superb new viewpoint. There will almost certainly be nobody else there. For once, instead of rushing up to Wasdale Head with the crowds, try Buckbarrow.

Park just to the right of the Greendale Restaurant which is on the Wasdale–Gosforth road, directly below Buckbarrow itself (grid ref. 144056). From here a green track rises up the fellside just to the right of the beck, which is itself rushing down to the right of the great buttresses of Buckbarrow. This leads easily to a wide gorge, where a yew tree has managed to obtain a secure hold in the screes, and to a shallow amphitheatre. Beyond here the path becomes stonier for a while, then leads out between more open and rolling fells. Quite suddenly Greendale Tarn is seen ahead, a lonely sheet of water cradled in a wide bowl, with steep, rocky ground rising on the right to the western slopes of Middle Fell and long, grassy but

Buckbarrow seen across Greendale

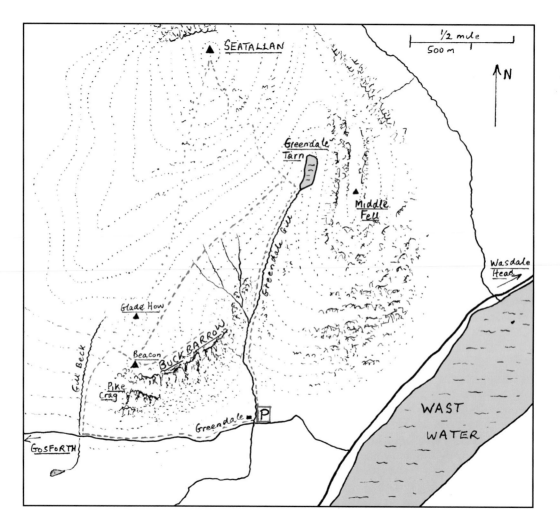

boulder-strewn slopes leading towards the higher top of Seatallan in the north-west.

For the purist – and those with enough time and energy to spend an additional hour or so on the trip – Seatallan is the logical high-ground to gain now and the reward for the effort is a splendid view over the long ridge of Yewbarrow, right into Hollow Stones and Scafell's precipices. But I do admit that it can seem a long and tedious grind battling up those pathless gradients to reach a top that never seems to arrive. A bit of variety makes all the difference in wild country and there isn't much on the tramp up to Seatallan.

Much more appealing is the prospect of simply contouring across the fellside towards where you know Buckbarrow's cliffs must be, even though you can't really see them from here. From the outflow of the waters from Greendale Tarn, the view back over the left shoulder towards Buckbarrow shows an obvious rocky beacon on the skyline and this now should be kept in view as you strike across the grassy but rough fellside towards it. There's no path – but choosing your own way is part of the charm of a walk like this. The rocky beacon is not marked on the map but is somewhere near the south-west end of the line of Buckbarrow's buttresses, near the point marked Pike Crag. So swing north-east (left) on leaving the beacon, and do wander along their tops from one little rocky lump to another for the views from them, across and along Wast Water and with the great crags dropping away at your feet, are really stunning.

When it is time to leave, head back towards the rocky beacon and then go further west again, towards Gill Beck, to avoid a very steep descent down the crags. Then a grassy path will be seen leading down to the Wasdale–Gosforth road, and an easy, downhill stroll along this soon leads back to where you left the car at the start of the walk.

The Scafells and Wastwater seen from Buckbarrow

30. *Latterbarrow and Whin Rigg*

Best Map: OS 1:25,000 S.W. Sheet (Wast Water and Coniston)

Distance: 5 miles/8km approx.

Highest elevation reached: 1755ft/535m

Height gained: 1500ft/457m

Overall star rating: *

General level of exertion required: Medium/high

Time for the round: 1 hour (Latterbarrow only) or 3½ hours

Terrain: Good path, rough fell, good path, steep and roughish descent – in that order. Latterbarrow on its own (just about 400ft/ 122m of ascent) gives a fine short easy walk in almost any weather.

I tried hard to work out a good circular way to the tops above the Wastwater Screes that would start in Boot in Eskdale, climb to Boat How by way of the Bronze Age stone circles and cairns up there and go on to Illgill Head, but the dreadful toil of the dreary fellside out of Miterdale, and the necessity to ford streams as well as climb fences, made me look for an alternative. I was pleased therefore to spot the fine little hill and splendid viewpoint of Latterbarrow which gives a good springboard to Whin Rigg. Here again, if you come across any crowds, they'll be of sheep, not of humans.

Park at grid ref. 129038: there is good parking for a few cars in the triangle of secondary roads between Forest Bridge over the Irt, and Cinderdale Bridge, just east of the village of Strands (Nether Wasdale on some maps). Now cross back over Forest Bridge and take the path signed for Eskdale at the side of the house called 'Flass'. This leads across a meadow through mature pine trees and over a stile to join a track alongside a wall. The slopes of Latterbarrow are now ahead on the right. The map suggests that Latterbarrow is covered by conifers; in fact, a considerable amount of timber has been felled, so the terrain is much more open than you might expect. Go over another stile and into the plantation area. The aim now is the summit of Latterbarrow so keep right when the track forks and then in another twenty yards left (on the main branch) until it starts to skirt round the foot of the hill to the left. Then you should take another track which slants right across the slope, much more obviously heading in the right direction. Just before reaching the summit rocks, with their little

Latterbarrow and Whin Rigg on the right, with the Wast Water Screes in shadow

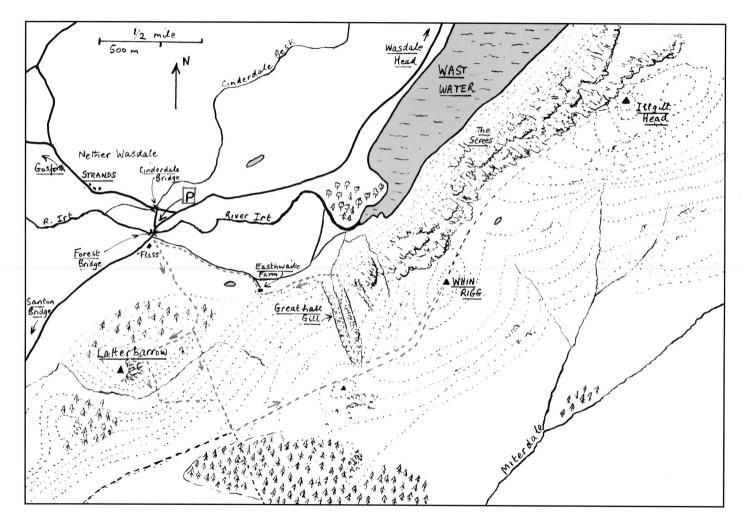

topknot of wind-blown pines, the track peters out and there's a final short scramble before a splendid view along the length of Wast Water.

Now either return or grit your teeth for the next section which involves descending the grassy slopes to the depression between Latterbarrow and the Whin Rigg ridge, dodging some ankle-breaking grass tussocks in a wet bog, then avoiding a wall with a fence, before tackling the open fell leading upwards. There's no obvious sign of the Eskdale path marked so clearly on the map until you near the ridge itself, with its walled-off conifer plantation. You then intersect with the path you need which leads north-east and climbs steadily up the broad-backed moor, over a stile and onto the open fell. Coming over a hump, there's the path curving up the last rise to Whin Rigg – the top! Just before tackling this, the path skirts the top of a chasm, a great slash in the fellside; this is called Greathall Gill and is the way down, so take note of it. Press on up the last slope and enjoy wandering along the line of shattered crags above The Screes where there are curious slips in the land, strange tips and tilts, a great prow of rock thrusting out over Wast Water, and – if you've chosen the right day – dramatic views along the line of cliffs to the cluster of peaks at the head of the lake.

Return now to Greathall Gill and descend a grassy tongue down its centre and then a sketchy path which winds down round shattered rock pinnacles and below crags of crumbly rock. The path isn't marvellous but it's adequate until you reach the tree-line where the

View across Greendale to the Wast Water Screes

stream tumbles over in a little waterfall and into a tree-girt gorge below. Now it is best to follow the track beaten out by the sheep, which contours away to the right to meet with the main descent path from Whin Rigg, marked on the map but much less interesting. At the bottom of the gill, either climb the stiles straightaway to join the farm track heading westwards back to the start, or, since it is easier underfoot, go left along a grassy footpath across fields to Easthwaite Farm. Then climb a stile to pass through the farmyard to join the last section of the track and so complete the round.

31.   Wallowbarrow

Best Map: OS 1:25,000 S.W. Sheet (Wast Water and Coniston)

Distance: 3½ miles/5.6km approx.

Highest elevation reached: 947ft/289m

Height gained: 600ft/183m

Overall star rating: * * *

General level of exertion required: Medium/low

Time for the round: 2½ hours

Terrain: Mostly good paths if you stick to the obvious route; some more adventurous and exciting rough country if you don't.

The valley of the River Duddon has sadly been a battleground between the Forestry Commission and various conservation bodies – the National Park, the National Trust and that excellent watchdog, The Friends of the Lake District – and the Forestry Commission has won too many of the contests. This is one of the most beautiful areas of the Lake District where, although there is no lake, there is a delightful stream which winds among fields, around small rocks

and large mountains. The scenery is lovely everywhere except where the regimented conifers clothe the eastern flanks of Harter Fell. I find these exasperating because they rarely have any glades as in natural mixed woodland, they cut off so much light that there's virtually no other vegetation and therefore little wildlife. Their close-packed trunks allow no views, and I suspect that most of their timber simply goes to add to the ridiculous bulk and weight that our Sunday newspapers in particular have now reached. No wonder the wind always 'sighs' in the conifers.

There are good and longer walks to be found in this area but the one I particularly enjoy is fairly short and, you'll not be surprised to learn, keeps out of the plantations as much as possible.

There is limited parking directly opposite the chapel in the tiny village of Seathwaite (grid ref. 229962), or find a spot in the village and walk to the chapel. Directly opposite the chapel is a public footpath sign pointing through a narrow stile and the path goes round a bend of the Tarn Beck for a short way, before crossing it by a footbridge. Another sign now points to another footbridge across the River Duddon itself and the path winds gently through meadow and woodland to reach it, then continues on towards High Wallowbarrow Farm. I prefer to turn right just after crossing this bridge and then scramble

Harter Fell seen from Wallowbarrow Crag

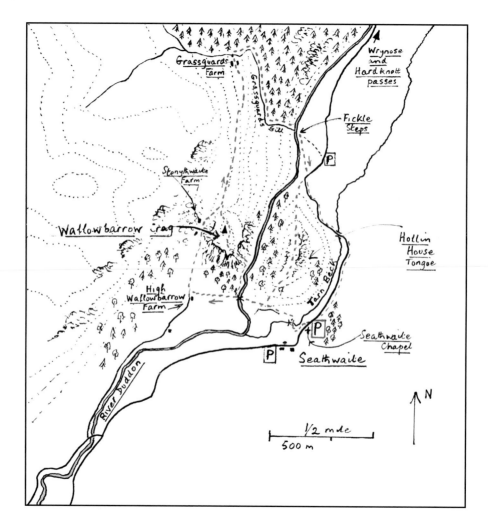

leftwards up the line of the wall that is almost immediately reached, because it gives a simple but most enjoyable climb with no difficulty right to the top of the excellent viewpoint of Wallowbarrow Crag. If this sounds a bit too adventurous for you, continue on the obvious path to the farm via a couple of gates, then climb gently past Stonythwaite Farm. That way skirts under the splendid crag instead. But don't fail to scramble to the top of Wallowbarrow for the view to the patchwork of fields down the dale and up it to the rugged shape of that wonderful little mountain, Harter Fell, and many other rocky heights with their attractive woods and tumbling becks.

The track now leads between the particularly fine stone walls built by the Sawrey family to Grassguards Farm. Cross the beck here by the ford or a footbridge and, on its far bank, turn right down Grassguards Gill, on the edge of the conifer plantation. This leads soon to the rather exciting crossing of the River Duddon again, at Fickle Steps, where a wire hawser safeguards the passage across the large stepping-stones in the river. On the other side bear right on the footpath that winds along through woods, climbing slowly above the river bank to reach the road. You may now either wander down the road itself to Seathwaite again, or take this alternative route. In fifty paces you'll reach a cattle-grid and a gate, and beyond that a sketchy path winds up the rocky hump of Hollin House Tongue. The path disappears, but the top of this rocky hillock gives a fine viewpoint.

You'll have now to find your own way down to

The Coniston Fells from Hollin House Tongue

Seathwaite. The wall is broken in a few places but where the sheep go so can you. Curve round left after crossing it, and you'll soon pick up the path along which you first started on your way to cross the Duddon and the end of a marvellous short walk.

32. Border End and Hard Knott

Best Map: OS 1:25,000 S.W. Sheet (Wast Water and Coniston)

Distance: 4 miles/6.4km approx.

Highest elevation reached: 1803ft/550m

Height gained: 1100ft/335m

Overall star rating: */**

General level of exertion required: Medium

Time for the round: About 2½ hours

Terrain: A rough path, then open fell, mostly pathless. It's not really a very good walk for a day of poor visibility, but it would be splendid on a day of *wild* weather.

The Hardknott Pass is well known, climbing in fierce hairpin-bends from the Duddon Valley over to Eskdale, but the fine fells above the pass are much less frequented. This short walk, like so many on these lower fells, is done by very few people and so gives a splendid taste of unspoiled and wild country. On a day of clear visibility, it has the additional attraction of wonderful views towards the Scafell massif and to Bowfell. The walk proposed is a 'triangular round': stalk the fell along its flank, then creep up on it and finally descend the steep side. The fact that the start-point is at 700 feet above sea level reduces the actual ascent involved to only 1100 feet.

The best place to park is just off the road about 300 yards beyond the gate at Cockley Beck Bridge at the bottom of the climb up to Hardknott Pass (grid ref. 242017). From here cross the stream and find the path that curves round to meet Mosedale and then goes up the left side of the depression down which the Mosedale Beck flows. Mosedales in the Lake District all tend to be a bit dreary and I suppose this one is no exception, but for me – so long as it's clear – this particular Mosedale is always an exciting one because of the tantalising glimpses to be seen ahead, beyond the watershed, to Esk Buttress (known as such to generations of climbers but called Dow Crag by the OS), and Pen (the little rocky summit above it), to Ill Crag and Scafell Pike.

The path is stony for a while and then dodges about a little to avoid boggy stretches, but it is clearly heading for the hause curving across the skyline which cuts off the view into Upper Eskdale. On the approach, keep to the left of its lowest point until the path disappears in another boggy patch. It reappears again shortly, but then trends away downhill to the

View to Border End from the Roman fort on Hard Knott

141

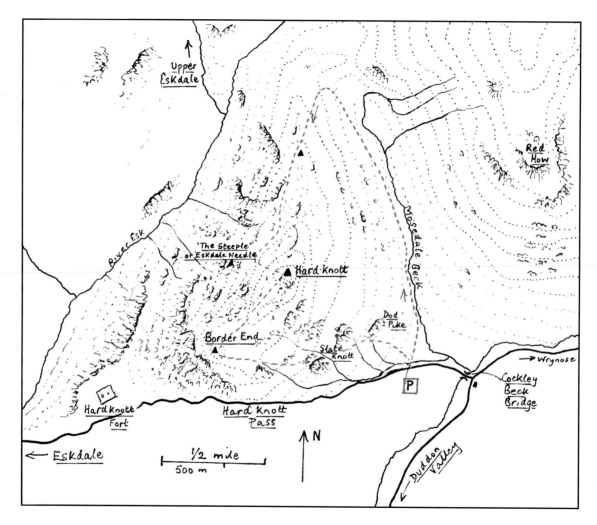

Upper
Eskdale

Red
How

River Esk

Mosedale Beck

'The Steeple'
or Eskdale Needle

Hard Knott

Dod
Pike

Border End

Slate
Knott

Wrynose

P

Cockley
Beck
Bridge

Hard Knott
Fort

Hard Knott
Pass

← Eskdale

½ mile

500 m

N

Duddon Valley

left and towards Eskdale, so you should now swing further left on the col and go due south up the grassy slopes towards the rocky lump on the skyline which has a cairn on its top. Beyond and ahead lie a line of ice-scoured, rocky humps to which you can now make your way, winding over and along them, peering over into Eskdale and back towards the fine view of Bowfell. Before trending to the left and visiting the highest fell – Hard Knott itself – you may choose to look for Eskdale Needle (also called The Steeple). This is indicated on the maps, though not very precisely. You may see it and not see it, if you get what I mean. Or you may wander around for some time searching for it, as I did three times before deciding that I'd finally found it. For in truth, it's really only a large rocky spike, seen by looking down a wide grassy gully on the Eskdale side of the ridge, just before the last pull up to the cairn on Hard Knott, and it's certainly not in the same class as Napes Needle on Gable. It's the view to the superb Upper Eskdale with its wild gorges, drumlins, crags and peaks that makes this walk so memorable.

Continue over a succession of rock outcrops, with odd cairns all over the place, to Border End where the fell drops abruptly to the valley. The remains of the Roman fort further down the pass cannot be seen from here because the fellside is convex, but you can catch a glimpse of it as you contour a little before beginning the descent of the slopes to the south-east. Obviously you can descend to the Hardknott Pass road itself if you choose, but it is much more in keeping with the

rest of this tramp to choose your own line down the steep fellside, well above the road, along the line of the craggy outcrops at Slate Knott and Dod Pike and so back to the start.

Esk Pike, Bowfell and the Crinkle Crags from Border End

143

33. High Gait Crags

Best Map: OS 1:25,000 S.W. Sheet (Wast Water and Coniston)

Distance: 7½ miles/12km approx.

Highest elevation reached: 1700ft/518m

Height gained: 1400ft/427m

Overall star rating: * * *

General level of exertion required: High/medium

Time for the round: 4–5 hours

Terrain: Good paths into Upper Eskdale, then rough fell. Fair paths on the return, becoming good. Not a walk for bad weather conditions.

This walk goes into the most magnificent cirque of high mountains in the Lake District and climbs to the high land in its centre, thus allowing close-up views of the great cliffs of Esk Buttress (Dow Crag on OS), Ill Crags and of course England's highest mountain, Scafell Pike, 1500 feet higher. The approach is up Eskdale: it takes some effort to get there and that is what protects this wonderful sanctuary from over-use, but anyone who appreciates high-mountain scenery simply must go.

There is a car park at grid ref. 213012, just uphill of the cattle-grid at the bottom of Hardknott Pass, or lay-bys a little further down Eskdale. Take the track towards Brotherilkeld Farm but just before the farm gates, bear left towards the River Esk. From here you can just see the summit of Scafell Pike peeping over the top of the surrounding fells and for once really looking like a peak. A signed footpath leads along the right bank beside sheep-pasture and, with Bowfell now fully in view ahead, through more fields, until the intake wall is left at a ladder-stile. Keep on, with the fine rampart of Yew Crags high above on the right, then the steep rocks of Heron Crag on the left and always the sound of running water from the river with its lovely pools of blue-green water, until the path swings left and, in addition to the cone of Bowfell, a new line of crinkled fells can be seen to its left. This is the skyline of Esk Pike and our objective, High Gait Crags, is in the middle-distance below it.

The white waters of two cascades in the Lingcove Beck, at its junction with the River Esk, are also visible ahead, and here an arched bridge leads over to the tongue of land between both streams. Go up the main path beside the Esk, here thundering down a rocky defile concealing many a lovely pool, but, after only a few yards, climb a fainter path up the left bank of Lingcove Beck. Reaching more level ground, the

Looking up Eskdale from the slopes above Brotherikeld Farm

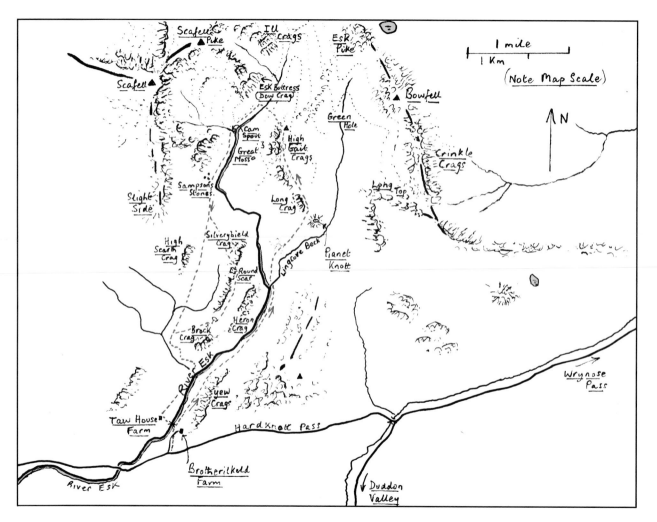

Scafell Pike

I.U Crags

Esk Pike

Scafell

Esk Buttress
Dow Crag

Bowfell

1 mile
1 Km
(Note Map Scale)

N

Green
Hole

Crinkle
Crags

Cam
Spout

High
Gait
Crags

Great
Moss

Slight
Side

Sampsons
Stones

Long
Crag

Long Top

High
Scarth
Crag

Silverybield
Crag

Lingcove Beck

Planet
Knott

Round
Scar

Heron
Crag

Brock
Crag

River ESK

Yew
Crags

Wrynose
Pass

Taw House
Farm

Hardknott Pass

River Esk

Brotherilkeld
Farm

Duddon
Valley

rocky lump of Pianet Knott is seen, framed between Bowfell and the extended skyline of Long Top on Crinkle Crags. Keep on towards this – there isn't really a path now – and then, rounding a little shoulder, the line of cliffs of Long Crag appears to the left of Pianet Crag, with a grassy hause between them, and this now becomes the objective. Once there, you've reached a long ridge curving round towards Esk Pike, with the basin of Green Hole (below the Crinkles and Bowfell), on your right and – as becomes very clear as you gain height up the ridge over Long Crag – the tremendous sweep of Upper Eskdale on your left. A little further and a tiny cairn on High Gait Crags is reached. The only sound is of rushing water echoing from the great crags; the clouds march overhead and the light and shade flit across the screes and precipices . . . And the view! I will not rave on about it. I think it's the finest in the Lake District.

To return, head downhill and ford the infant River Esk, well above the flat and boggy area of the Great Moss, and make for the drier path below the steep crag of Esk Buttress and past the cascade of Cam Spout. This now leads behind the isolated rocks called Sampson's Stones, through a sheepfold, up on to the fell away from the bends in the River Esk and winds along the depression between Silverybield Crag on the left and the steep little knot of High Scarth Crag on the right. It is a straightforward way back from here, but just a little more effort will take you across the depression to the high land on its left edge, a line of rocky tops running from Round Scar to Brock

Crag which will give more marvellous views back to Slight Side and Scafell Pike.

At the end of this ridge is the path again, winding down quickly now at the side of the gill to a farm track at a bridge by a fine little waterfall. Follow the track to Taw House Farm, and from the yard a stile leads to the path and the footbridge back to Brotherilkeld.

Esk Buttress and Ill Crags seen from High Gait Crags

147

34. Harter Fell

Best map: OS 1:25,000 S.W. Sheet (Wast Water and Coniston)

Distance: 5 miles/8km

Highest elevation reached: 2129ft/649m

Height gained: 1830ft/558m

Overall star rating: * * *

General level of exertion required: Medium/high

Time for the round: About 3 hours

Terrain: On good or fair paths for the ascent; the descent is not so obvious, is rougher and boggier, so reasonable visibility is desirable.

Harter Fell is one of the wildest, rockiest, most distinctive and finest summits in the Lake District and yet still seems to be remarkably little visited. This walk starts in Eskdale, climbs to the summit by the west flank and returns via the top of the Hardknott Pass. There are two alternative starts.

Park at the bottom of the Hardknott Pass near the gateway to Brotherilkeld Farm or just uphill of the cattle-grid (grid ref. 213012). Cross the stream by a footbridge, where there used to be a ford, and take the upper path which now slants gently at first and then more steeply to the south-west, curving round the flank of the fell to the watershed between Harter Fell and the line of craggy tops towards Ulpha Fell in the west. Before reaching the hause, another path, well marked with plenty of cairns, goes left, taking a zigzag line alongside a broken rocky rib towards the top, then curving round to the right to avoid some little crags and back left to the three cones, two of which are higher than the third, that crown this particular rocky summit.

Alternatively, you may find parking easier at grid ref. 203009, near Whahouse Bridge where there are some lay-bys, and then take the bridleway immediately on the east side of the bridge. This leads across a field to a ladder-stile at which turn left and follow the path up either side (though normally on the left/east) of the obvious gill: this is not named on the map though I believe it is called Spothow Gill. Its steep ravine comes straight down the fellside towards you. Near its top, bear left and cross a fence by a stile beside a wall and the main path or bridleway coming from Hard Knott to Grassguards is then joined. It is then to the top as described above.

The summit of Harter Fell has the reputation of being the only one in Lakeland which cannot be ascended without using hands as well as feet – which

Harter Fell seen from Eskdale

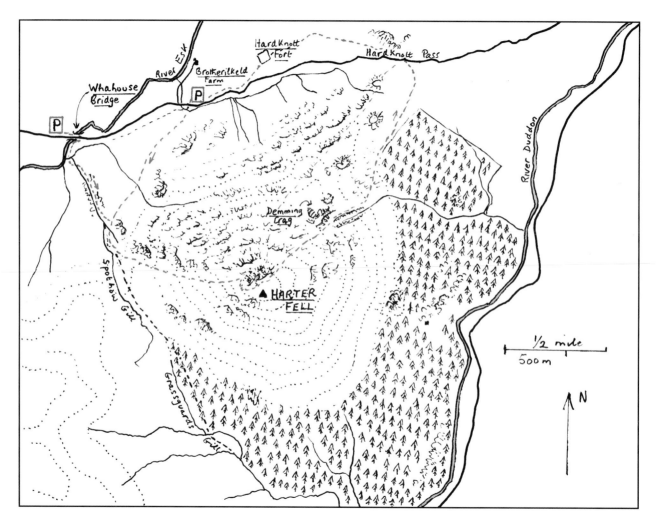

River Esk

Hard Knott Fort

Hard Knott Pass

Whahouse Bridge

Brotherikeld Farm

P

P

Spothow Gill

Demming Crag

HARTER FELL

River Duddon

Grassguards Gill

½ mile

500m

N

no doubt is the reason why the OS triangulation point is a few feet lower and a few yards away from the rocky platform of the highest point. The truth doesn't quite live up to the reputation, but it's not very easy with hands in pockets. However you get there, it is a superb place to stand and look around in all directions at a marvellous panorama of high fells, particularly of course to the wild landscape of the Scafell massif at the head of Eskdale. By changing position a little, you can have a fine aerial view of the remains of the Roman fort on the slopes about halfway up the pass and imagine the Roman soldiers being marched about on a parade-ground.

The descent to Hardknott Pass can go down the not very obvious path which heads firstly just a little to the east to avoid steep rock and then north-east towards the conifer plantations crawling up the fell-side from the Duddon Valley. The path goes down towards Demming Crag and along the edge of a little ravine to its right, becoming more obvious as a stile leads over a fence next to the plantation and then cairns define the way as far as the top of the Hard-knott Pass. Alternatively, you do now have a golden opportunity for some real fellwalking, choosing your own way down. You'll be dodging around little crags, finding little hidden tarns, wandering over bracken, bogs, grass, rock and heather – where it seems no human foot has ever been before. Marvellous!

Once you reach the pass, turn down the road, but only as far as the first hairpin, after which you can walk down the fellside towards the walls of

the fort. To sit there quietly on a calm evening as the sun goes down and just absorb the atmosphere of this remarkably-situated place can be a very moving experience.

Your start-point is, of course, now just down the road or, if parked near Whahouse, cross the foot-bridge by the cattle-grid and then take the lower path alongside the wall and so back to Whahouse Bridge.

View from the slopes of Harter Fell to the Scafell group, with the Roman fort in the foreground

35.   Green Crag and Stanley Force

Best Map: OS 1:25,000 S.W. Sheet (Wast Water
    and Coniston)

Distance: 7½ miles/12 km approx.

Highest elevation reached: 1602ft/488m

Height gained: 1350ft/411m

Overall star rating: * * *

General level of exertion required: Medium/high

Time for the round: About 4 hours

Terrain: A fairly obvious ascent up a gill but then
    really wild, rough and rocky fell. Return along
    a lovely wooded valley bottom. Route-finding
    in a mist on the open fell could give a few
    problems.

The modest height gained on this walk can easily disguise the fact that it goes over some of the wildest and roughest ground in this book, as well as the most gentle. There is a tremendous contrast between the lovely green and wooded fields of Eskdale, with its river winding through them, and the rugged and rocky line of minor summits which form its southern rampart, to the west of Harter Fell. Every time I drove through Eskdale I wondered about those rocky tors and at last I went to see for myself. How did I ever miss this walk for all these years!

Park somewhere near Whahouse Bridge (grid ref. 203009) in Eskdale, not far from the bottom of the Hardknott Pass; there are various spots along the roadside. The objective now is to attain the saddle between Harter Fell on your left hand and the line of rocky humps further to the right (west). A gill (unnamed on my map but which I believe is Spothow Gill, and very obvious from Whahouse Bridge) leads south-south-west in precisely this direction and is reached by taking the bridleway just on the east side of the bridge and then the path over a couple of stiles up the right bank of the ravine (as you look up it) which climbs steeply through beautiful mixed woodland.

As the trees come to an end, the path – by now very sketchy – crosses the stream to reach a stile over a wire fence beside the wall and joins the good bridleway which leads from the bottom of Hardknott Pass over to Grassguards in the Duddon Valley. It is now a steady uphill tramp until, just beyond a long rocky spur leading to Harter Fell, the path forks. Keep right and then, before reaching the watershed, make your way over the wire fence, through grass and

*Spothow Gill below
Harter Fell*

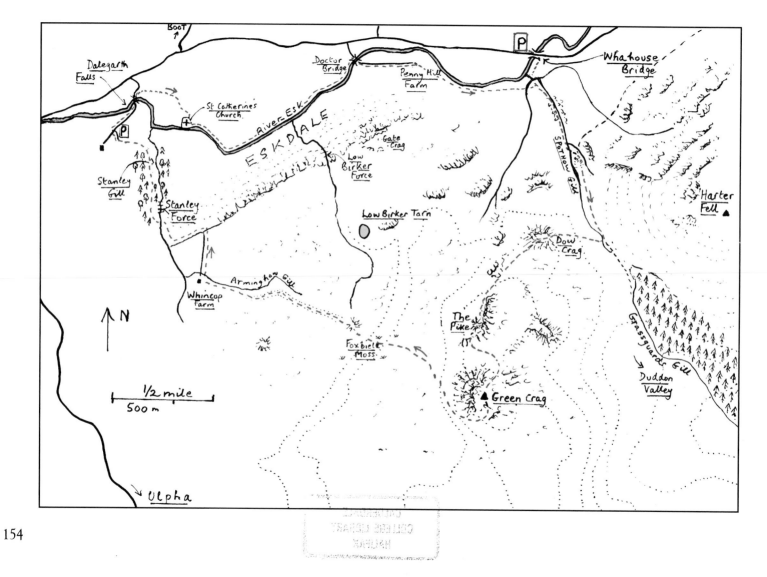

bracken and then through heather, towards the line of jagged little peaks on the right. This is rough fell now, but you can scramble along all the rocky places in an arc, swinging from Dow Crag to the sharp eminence of The Pike and eventually to the fine viewpoint on Green Crag.

Descend from here initially to the south (there's a lot of good scrambling rock round the other side) and then, when below the crags, head generally north-west towards Low Birker Tarn on a very sketchy path. You will soon be crossing Foxbield Moss and the firmer ground of the rocks in its middle will be welcome drier land for a little while. Just beyond the rocks and well before reaching the tarn, swing sharply west (left) where a vague sort of track leads along Arminghow Gill to meet a path at Whincop Farm. Turn away from the farm, go alongside a wall to a large stile near a corner, then double back left alongside the other wall on a path which soon leads to the well-trodden one at the head of Stanley Gill. (If you are short of time, you can just go straight on downhill, but you will miss two of the most interesting parts of the walk.)

Stanley Force is a really fine cascade – and you may see the Eskdale Outward Bound team 'doing a tyrolean' (which is pulling yourself on a rope) across the gorge. Nearly at the foot of the gill, follow the signs for Eskdale Green, over the river bridge by Dalegarth Falls and then, just before reaching the main road, turn right along the track between ancient stone walls, signed for the simple but beautifully situated

Harter Fell seen from Green Crag

church of St Catherine beside the river. The church-yard contains a masterpiece in rock in the tombstone of Tommy Dobson, Master of Foxhounds. Doctor Bridge is not far away now, reached by a delightful path alongside the stream, and you're soon looking across to Birker Force spouting over the ramparts of Gate Crag. Cross the Esk by the bridge, reach Penny Hill Farm and continue across the pasture until the track enters a wood, crosses a gill, and Whahouse Bridge is only a stone's throw away.

155

36.   Red How and Cold Pike

Best Map: OS 1:25,000 S.W. Sheet (Wast Water and Coniston)

Distance: 3 miles/4.8km or 4½ miles/7.2km

Highest elevation reached: 2426ft/739m or 2259ft/689m

Height gained: 1000ft/305m or 1700ft/518m

Overall star rating: *

General level of exertion required: Tough if Red How is included, otherwise medium

Time for the round: 2½ hours, 3½ hours or more for the longer distance

Terrain: Fair paths on high fells, but plenty of rough ground if you choose the longer option.

Red How and Cold Pike are tops on the great curving northern wall of the Wrynose Pass called Wrynose Breast and you get a sight of them just peeping over the top of the fell as you look up the pass from Cockley Beck Bridge. That they aren't particularly obvious tops doesn't mean that they aren't worth climbing: it is simply that they aren't noticed so much, except by fell-runners. You can cheat a bit by driving up to the top of the Wrynose Pass which is at 1281ft above sea level to start with, and then climb all of 978ft fairly directly to Cold Pike and tell yourself you've been on a big fell, which you have, but you've only made about as much effort as you would if you go up Silver How. If that appeals to you, then it's very easy to tell you what to do.

Park on the roadside at the top of the Wrynose Pass near the Three Shire Stone (where Lancashire, Cumberland and Westmorland used to meet – and still do for many old-timers – grid ref. 277027). Then take the obvious path which leads north-westwards directly from the stone, up the right side of the depression, crossing several little becks en route and with the main stream of Roughcrags Gill well to the left. In a little under a mile of steady upward progress, you reach Red Tarn nestling between the high ground of Pike o' Blisco on the right hand and that of Cold Pike on the left. Here you meet the main path climbing from Great Langdale and, as it swings west and slants across the slopes of Cold Pike on its way towards Great Knott and the Crinkles, you may as well join it for a way, to the point where the main path curves right as it crosses the little beck at the very head of Browney Gill. Now head south instead of north-west and a gentle ascent up grassy and boulder-strewn slopes (no path, just the odd sheep track) soon

Cockley Beck, with Red How and Cold Pike beyond

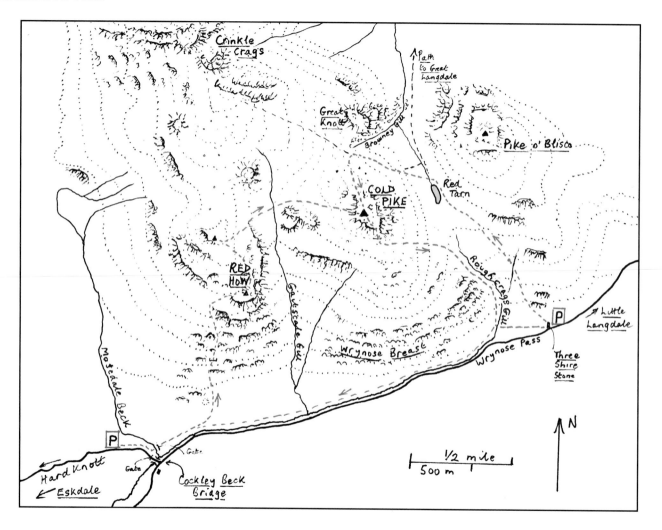

leads to the several very rocky summits of Cold Pike itself. The views to Swirl How and Wetherlam are particularly good.

The descent is equally straightforward for there is a reasonable path, easily found by heading east across the slopes overlooking the Wrynose Pass and marked by cairns. This quickly leads downhill and eventually crosses Roughcrags Gill to gain the road again and the Three Shire Stone. That's the short way, and it's a good one.

The longer and tougher walk is for those who are prepared to start at Cockley Beck Bridge, 700ft lower and a good deal further away, where the Hard Knott road meets Wrynose (grid ref. 247017). Their reward is the pleasure, and pain, of a virtually trackless ascent. (The OS maps show a footpath but you will be hard-pressed to find it.) Assuming that virtually virgin ground appeals to you as it does to me, start by crossing the Hard Knott road bridge and then fording the Mosedale Beck on stones. Now go through the gate and over bracken-covered moor towards the slopes of Red How and a prominent nick in the skyline, which has a long grassy rake slanting roughly towards it. Halfway up the fell, a gate leads through a wall and it is then a stiff climb over tussocky grass, with very good optional scrambling on the perfect rock outcrops. Veer left to avoid a steep rampart of reddish rock and then, with more splendid little rock scrambles, reach Red How. A lower cairn leads to a higher one to the north, and then a curving line

Wetherlam from Cold Pike

around the head of a wide and boggy depression leads on to Cold Pike.

Follow the path down from there to the top of Wrynose as described for the shorter walk, and then walk down the pass to return to Cockley Beck; I've tried the alternative of descending the Cold Pike slopes directly towards Cockley Beck and it is simply not worth it.

37.   Yewdale Fells

Best Map: OS 1:25,000 S.W. Sheet (Wast Water and Coniston)

Distance: 5–6 miles/8–9.6km

Highest elevation reached: 1345ft/410m

Height gained: 1050ft/320m (but *see* below)

Overall star rating: * *

General level of exertion required: Medium/high (because of the 700ft/213m climb on the return)

Time for the round: 3½–4 hours

Terrain: A good mixture of well-used paths, sheep tracks and fairly rough fellwalking

An ancient, original and well-used path crosses the edge of the Yewdale Fells, linking Coniston's Coppermines Valley with the attractive Tilberthwaite Gill, but it reveals little of them. This walk crosses the fell in both directions and provides a very satisfying and interesting tramp.

About two miles north-east of Coniston, on the main A593 road to Ambleside, take the first secondary road on the left as far as the obvious car park at the end of Tilberthwaite Gill (grid ref. 306009). A path directly out of the car park winds up the left bank of the gill, initially beside disused slate quarries, until it forks. Here it is worth taking a short diversion to the right to view the ravine, with one footbridge leading quickly to another, and impressive glimpses of the inner sanctum of the gorge. You can't escape from the ravine so return to the left-hand path which leads above the depths and swings left onto open fell with the stream on your right. This path now winds roughly due south up a shallow depression below the long eastern slopes of Wetherlam, eventually descending into the Coppermines Valley, and this is the easiest way to go.

If you are in the mood for a spot of *real* fellwalking, head off the path, west from here, over trackless ground towards rocky heights ahead. These can be linked in an arc, leading to a large cairn on the most obvious, High Wythow, which also discloses a surprise view of Coniston Water and the village. Going west from here, past a rocky flat-topped height and another with a cairn, you'll soon have a fine view into the Coppermines Valley, and will join up with the path you left recently.

Use this path to descend to Church Beck and

Looking north from Yewdale Fells to Holme Fell

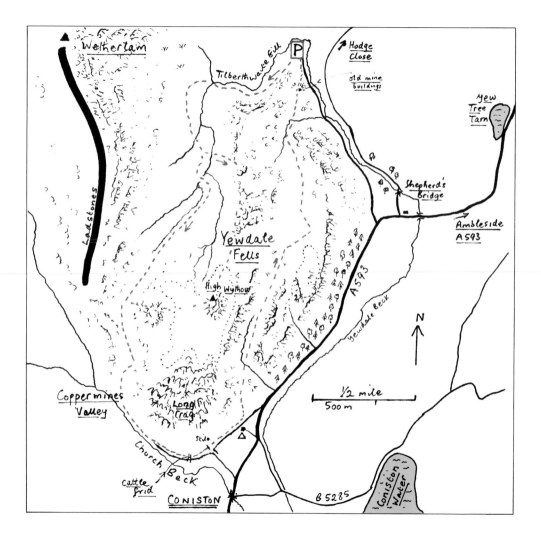

Wetherlam

Tilberthwaite Gill

P

Hodge Close

old mine buildings

Yew Tree Tarn

Shepherd's Bridge

Ambleside A593

Ladstones

Yewdale Fells

A593

Yewdale Beck

High Wythow

N

½ mile
500 m

Coppermines Valley

Long Crag

Church Beck

Stile

Cattle Grid

CONISTON

B 5285

Coniston Water

follow it down its left bank as far as a cattle-grid. In a further fifty paces, by the angle of a high wall, a stile leads left to a gentle green path just outside the wall. (Above and to the left, incidentally, is the fine buttress of Long Crag which gives several ways to the fell-tops for the competent scrambler.) Follow the green path for about three hundred paces until there is a gate in the wall on the right. Now look carefully for, though shown on the map, the narrow, grassy pathway that starts from here is easily missed. It slants to the right up the fellside, quickly becomes more distant, then gets a bit lost in an area of gorse bushes and where it crosses a little beck, then becomes clear again as it traverses just below the steep crags and makes for a shallow depression between a rim of rocky ground on the right and higher rough ground on the left. It sounds complicated, but it's a natural line and once a fairly high level is reached on the fell, the odd cairn makes route-finding easier. It was almost certainly a way used by miners working in Tilberthwaite but living in Coniston.

Towards the end of the fell-crossing, the path again becomes very indistinct. The Tilberthwaite valley is below, but rocky and steep fellside, defended by impenetrable-looking juniper, makes it advisable to keep high and to the left. Happily the path quickly reappears again, winding pleasantly down through a shallow ravine with rocky bluffs colonised by juniper. At its end, the path becomes a green track swinging right down to the valley floor; but ignore its change of direction, cross the stream and continue down a less

obvious path which quickly leads to a derelict slate-quarry and its tumbledown buildings. The road is now immediately below and the car park just around the corner.

The Coppermines Valley from Yewdale Fells

163

38. Lingmoor Fell

Best Map: OS 1:25,000 S.W. Sheet (Wast Water and Coniston)

Distance: Approx. 6 miles/9.6km

Highest elevation reached: 1530ft/466m

Height gained: 1250ft/381m

Overall star rating: * * *

General level of exertion required: Medium

Time for the round: 3–4 hours

Terrain: On good paths, though fairly rough between Brown Howe and Side Pike. Unless the mist is really low, this can be a good day in most weather conditions.

Lingmoor Fell separates Great Langdale from Little Langdale and this excellent walk goes through the trees that partly hide the slate-quarrying around Elterwater village and then, by good paths and green tracks, climbs to its spine. After an exhilarating stretch, with fine views of the head of Great Langdale, it descends to the valley floor, returning along the south side of Great Langdale Beck. (A shorter version, starting at the Blea Tarn car park (grid ref. 295045), which is almost 400ft higher than Elterwater, is possible and quite popular, but it does sacrifice a lot of the charm and variety of the walk now described and which I think is better.)

Getting the start right is important; thereafter the way is, or certainly should be, fairly obvious. Leave the National Trust car park in Elterwater (grid ref. 327047 which is perhaps conveniently almost opposite the Britannia Inn) or other suitable spots nearby. Cross Great Langdale Beck by the road bridge going south. Now immediately turn right (north-east) along the metalled road running alongside (and soon at a slightly higher level than) the river itself. After a short way, a signed footpath leads down to the river bank and then, without crossing the footbridge, swings away and climbs gently through a sort of slate cutting towards the great black sheds of the quarry works. (The footbridge you didn't cross leads to what used to be the Langdales Hotel but is now, since the marketing men got to work on it, called Wainwright's Inn.)

Follow footpath signs across the quarry yard to a tree-shaded lane at the far side. In a hundred paces or so, go immediately across the metalled track at the side of Crossgates Cottage and find a broad path

Lingmoor Fell seen from Blake Rigg, with Little Langdale Tarn and Windermere

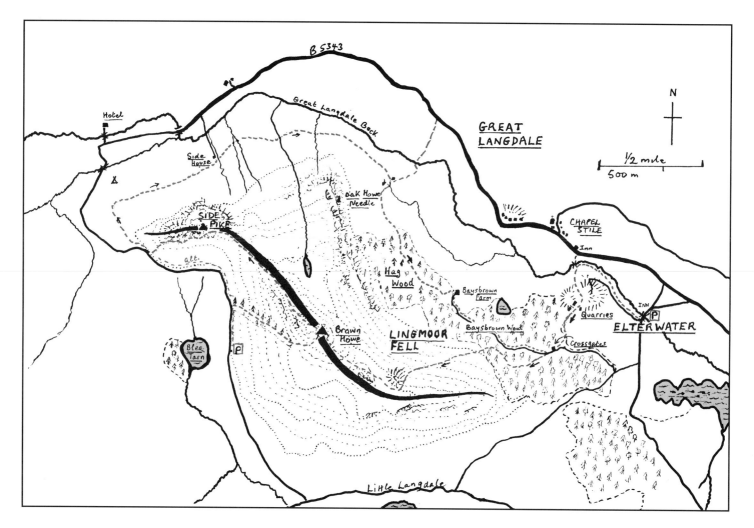

gently rising through the trees. Route-finding problems should now be over for this path gives a superb way uphill, threading between old spoil-heaps and slanting gently upwards. As it rises above the tree level, it zigzags up to a stile and then out onto the open fell just below the ridge itself. Now head to the right (north-west) round the upper side of some old workings and follow the line of the ridge. The path winds round rocky knolls and over the odd stile but there is a mounting sense of excitement as the cairn on Brown Howe (the highest point) is reached and, shortly beyond it, a splendid view of the Langdale Pikes.

The path, obviously more used than in the earlier section by those who have come up an alternative way, is now rough and rocky in places. It descends through the heather, which happily has not been taken over by the voracious bracken, alongside the summit wall and fence, towards the saddle beyond which rears up the steep rock wall of Side Pike. A diversion is clearly essential here and the path swings left directly under the crag, at one point squeezing behind a large rock, then contouring quite excitingly round the steep fellside beyond, before descending towards the road at its highest point where it breasts the rise out of Great Langdale. A large stile leads directly to the road on the pass itself but there is no need to use it. Veer to the right, parallel to the road, and follow the path that soon leads steeply downhill towards Great Langdale and the campsite in the valley bottom.

Just before reaching the campsite, swing right and follow the path over stiles and many little becks and rills, passing Side House, climbing slightly to avoid swampy ground and generally skirting well below the high crags where Oak Howe Needle can be seen, partly detached from the hillside. This is a delightful stretch of the walk, but avoid any tracks that do not keep well to the right-hand side of the valley floor until you pass through Hag Wood and so on to Baysbrown Farm, well known to summer campers. For the last stretch, through Baysbrown Wood, the track is metalled, leading back quickly to Crossgates Cottage where your outward route is rejoined.

The Langdale Pikes from Lingmoor Fell

39. Blake Rigg

Best Map: OS 1:25,000 S.W. Sheet (Wast Water and Coniston)

Distance: 3½ miles/5.6.km

Highest elevation reached: 1760ft/536m

Height gained: 1100ft/335m

Overall star rating: **/***

General level of exertion required: Fairly high

Time for the round: 2½–3 hours

Terrain: Grass, rock, grassy rakes; virtually no sign of footpaths on the fell itself, so it is not advisable to be wandering about on it in poor weather.

Blake Rigg is just west of Blea Tarn and its traverse gives a fine mountain day in miniature while allowing superb views of the Langdale skyline. It presents a steep and craggy face towards Little Langdale and this perhaps explains its apparent neglect. On one of my own very first visits to the Lake District, I camped amongst the trees above Blea Tarn (I don't suppose I'd get away with that nowadays!) and,

burdened with a huge rucksack, actually scrambled a route up these crags on my way to Bowfell. I shudder at the thought now. I recall dislodging lumps of moss and grass from the slimy chimney up which I struggled and pulling a huge flake of rock away. When it tumbled down the rock face to the grass and scree below, I nearly joined it. Fortunately I stayed wedged, while the smell of sulphur, which can usually be detected after a fall of rock, wafted up to me. This walk, of course, doesn't do anything desperate like that and certainly doesn't go directly up the crags.

The best start is the Blea Tarn car park at grid ref. 295045, which means a visit can be made to this well-known tarn in its lovely setting of pines and rhododendrons. Blea Tarn manages to survive the countless clicks of countless cameras and gives an ideal foreground for a view of the Langdale Pikes. Follow the good path around the west side and then, just before reaching the road again at the point where it descends steeply to Great Langdale, turn left through the gap in the wall and then follow the wall uphill. Almost immediately it fades into a little crag, so curve to the right to reach the broad and grassy ridge above and then upwards again, before a slight descent leads to a hause where the wall reappears. Choose your own way uphill now (which means of course that there isn't really any alternative), just

View to Blake Rigg from Little Langdale Tarn

169

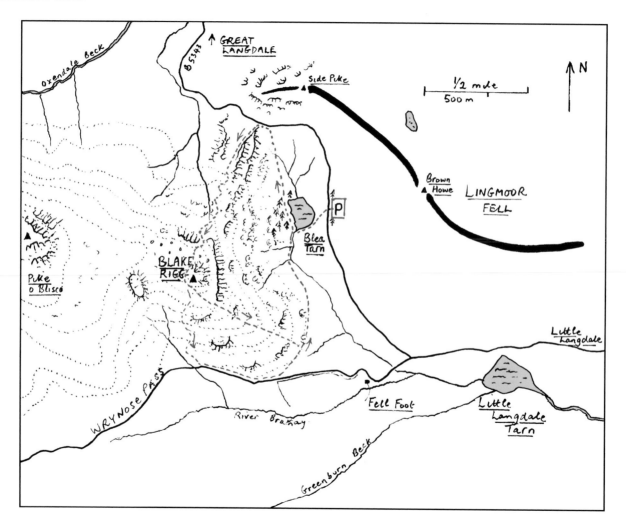

right of a line of larches, climbing over or around little rocky outcrops to a cairn on a rocky lump, which is on a level with the main sweep of crags on the left. Above here, a line of rock ribs gives good, easy scrambling – or follow grassy rakes round them – always going for the highest crags. This is my idea of fellwalking at its best: not too obvious a line, plenty of variation underfoot and away from well-worn paths. Because it is so absorbing, it certainly feels as if you've climbed a lot more than 1100ft.

Once attained, there are several cairned points on the broad summit ridge and an extraordinary number of little tarns trapped in rocky or grassy basins all around the area. From the highest cairn, follow the ridge over more rocky tops but heading gently down-hill now, choosing a line generally towards Wetherlam whose bulk looms large across Little Langdale. More adventurous and experienced fell-walkers may prefer to stay with the line of the ridge as it trends towards Little Langdale Tarn to complete the descent for, although it is steeper, it remains rockier and, in high summer and autumn at least, it is less hindered by bracken which can very effectively hide ankle-spraining holes.

An easier-angled descent is found by trending right to the lower part of the fell to reach the Wrynose Pass road seen below although, in summer, there is no evading the bracken, I'm afraid. The truth is that the descent is not particularly enjoyable, but it is soon over and it's worth enduring for the sake of the high quality of the walk as a whole. Before reaching the farm at Fell Foot, a finger-post points left across the foot of the fell to a footpath which, although not too obvious initially as it passes over some swampy ground, soon becomes clearer and then follows the contours northwards back to Blea Tarn to complete the circuit.

From the slopes of Blake Rigg: view over Kettle Crag to Bowfell

171

40. Tarn Crag (Easedale)

Best Map: OS 1:25,000 S.W. Sheet (Wast Water and Coniston) overlapping with S.E. Sheet (Windermere and Kendal)

Distance: 5 miles/8km approx.

Highest elevation reached: 1801ft/549m

Height gained: 1600ft/488m

Overall star rating: */* *

General level of exertion required: Fairly high

Time for the round: 3½–4 hours

Terrain: Fairly steep but grassy paths on the ascent to Tarn Crag and good, though at times stony, tracks for the rest of the way.

The walk up to Easedale Tarn from Grasmere is one of the most popular excursions on foot in the district, though for many people it seems to peter out when they get there. To climb up to Tarn Crag gives another, and very fine, objective and also enables a convenient return down the even more attractive Far Easedale.

Either park in Grasmere and walk up the Easedale road, or use the car park a little way up Easedale, just beyond Goody Bridge Farm, at grid ref. 334081, beyond which motoring is strictly and rightly restricted anyway. Continue up the road on foot, then cross the Easedale Beck on the left by the two footbridges (signed for Easedale Tarn). This way now leads across meadows, alongside a wall, over more meadows and then up the left bank of Sourmilk Gill, climbing past what can be most spectacular cascades of water, before the angle eases a little. The main path continues along the left bank of the tarn but, instead, go across to the outflow. Here there is a bit of excitement as you cross the water, using the natural stepping-stones – if they're not too deeply submerged. I have dithered here myself once or twice when it has looked a bit risky. When it is like that, you must walk further on, round the perimeter of the tarn, to reach much the same place on the far side.

Now strike up and left across the fellside on a reasonable path through bracken which climbs up to a grassy saddle on the spur running down from Tarn Crag itself, and then continue up the spur. The highest rocks of Tarn Crag are above and to the left of the fine profile of Deer Bields Crag, perched on the fellside and well seen from here; this is rock-climber's territory. It is now only a short but steep little climb up an open grassy gully to the highest ground. A walk

Tarn Crag on the left, and Deer Bields Crag

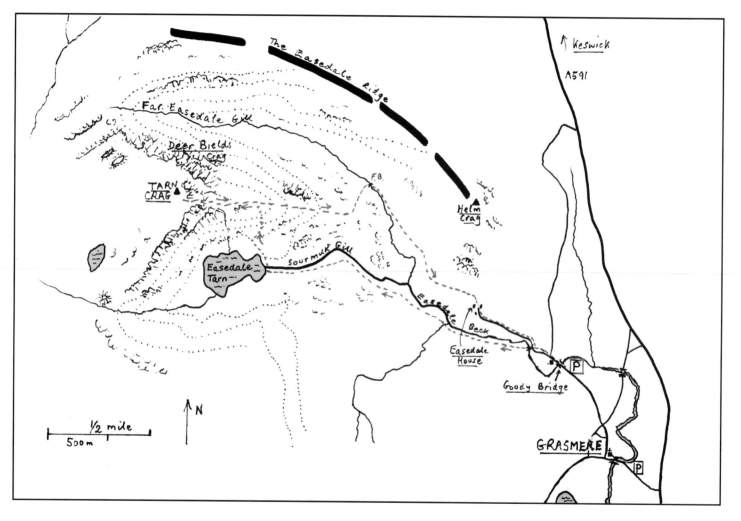

to another high-point on the left reveals not only an eagle's eye view of Easedale Tarn and the vale of Grasmere but also the rolling line of fine ridges with Helvellyn on the skyline. On one occasion when I was here, I met an elderly American couple busily taking snapshots of everything in sight; and I did have a laugh with them about the fact that they both wore badges with their names on (would you believe he was called Elmer?) and stating that they were from Washington DC. But they had certainly not just ambled to the tarn and back.

In the past, I have personally continued this walk by going along the ridge from here towards Sergeant Man and then descending to the head of Far Easedale, but it is a steady trudge along the rest of the broad ridge, it isn't too obvious where to descend and there are no views as good as those you've had already, so I feel that it is better now to descend from the summit back to the saddle.

There is then a cairned descent path towards the foot of the ridge, bearing well to the left, and actually backwards for a little way at the bottom, then leading over a wooden footbridge to cross the waters of Far Easedale Gill. (I don't suppose the enthusiasm will last, but on my last visit here I watched four young men alternately pedalling and carrying their mountain bikes up the rough Far Easedale track towards Borrowdale.) Once on the main path down Far Easedale, it is a straightforward, though at times quite rocky walk down this delightful valley, alongside the beck for quite a way and then between walls to reach

the metalled road again at Easedale House below Helm Crag. A short walk down the road soon sees you to the end of a delightful excursion.

Looking north to Helvellyn from Tarn Crag

41. Blea Rigg and Great Castle How

Best Map: OS 1:25,000 S.W. Sheet Wast Water
   and Coniston (overlapping with S.E. Sheet
   Windermere and Kendal)

Distance: 5½ miles/8.8km

Highest elevation reached: 1778ft/542m

Height gained: 1400ft/427m

Overall star rating: */**

General level of exertion required: Fairly high

Time for the round: 3½–4 hours

Terrain: Good or fair fell-paths for much of
   the way.

Great Castle How and Blea Rigg are tops on the south-western ridge of the cirque of fells cradling Easedale Tarn. But unless you see them from there very early in the morning, their crags are in shadow, they seem far away and look much more insignificant than is the case. This walk climbs up to their ridge to traverse and appreciate their fine situation, then descends to the tarn and returns down Sourmilk Gill. In so doing, it combines some wild landscape with a much-loved stroll through the Easedale meadows.

Park either in Grasmere village or up Easedale itself in the car park just before Goody Bridge Farm at grid ref. 334081 (it just isn't worth ignoring the 'No parking beyond this point' sign). A little further on, the road is gated on the bend and, just before reaching it, the footpath is signed to Easedale Tarn, over footbridges. Cross the beck and then the meadow, to go alongside the wall on the left for a hundred paces, keeping an eye open for the discreet sign, which can easily be missed, to 'Blindtarn Moss', beside a five-barred gate. This path leads straightforwardly across more meadow towards farm buildings, then through a gate at their left-hand side and onto the fell. The path is not too obvious here but follow the course of the beck uphill, swinging to the right just before reaching the wall ahead, when the way becomes clearer again. It now leads upwards through bracken and then through an extensive area of fine juniper bushes before reaching Blindtarn Moss which was clearly the site of a tarn before its retaining wall was breached. The path skirts the left-hand side of this boggy area and continues climbing still, not too distinctly in places but cairned, through the juniper and then up onto the broad, grassy col of the main ridge. Bear right now, over undulating grassy and rocky fell, climbing another couple of hundred feet to the more

The outlet of Easedale Tarn with Blea Rigg and Great Castle How

177

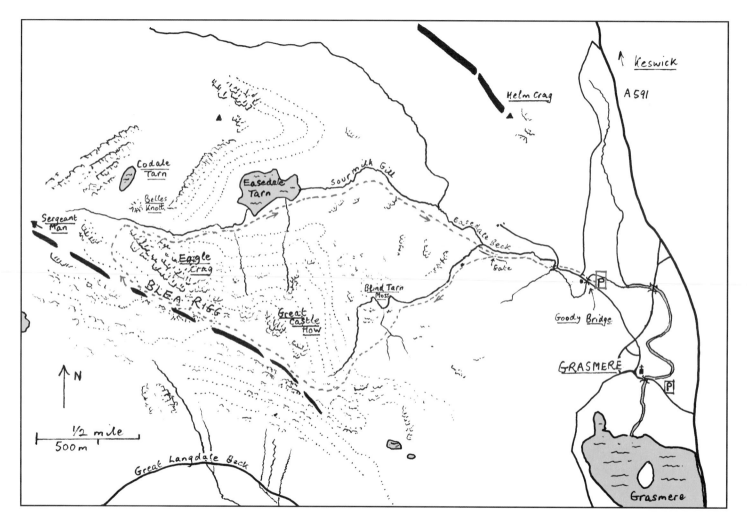

Keswick

A591

Helm Crag

Codale
Tarn

Easedale
Tarn

Sourmilk Gill

Belles
Knott

Easedale Beck

Sergeant
Man

Eagle
Crag

Gate

P

Goody Bridge

BLEA RIGG

Blind Tarn
Moss

Great
Castle
How

GRASMERE

P

N

½ mile
500 m

Great Langdale Beck

Grasmere

defined craggy area which is Great Castle How, overlooking Easedale, and you should see why it's worth coming up here – apart from the exercise, of course.

The path now twists and turns along the broad ridge and a short diversion to the west, left, will give views of the great cliffs of Pavey Ark and Harrison Stickle. Skirt small tarns on their right-hand sides before descending into a depression, and then climbing up and leaving the path for a while, to the complex of rock castles that make up Blea Rigg. Here you are high above the steep but verdant Eagle Crag, with the eagle's eye view of Easedale Tarn below and also of the much smaller Codale Tarn, glinting on a shelf behind the rocky lump of Belles Knott. There may be no eagles here now, but the cliffs are of little interest to rock-climbers and it is a wild and secluded enough fellside for peregrine falcons. I made at least five visits to these cliffs awaiting suitable lighting for photography and several times watched peregrines soar along the line of crags below me.

Now find the path again, continue towards the distant cone of Sergeant Man and look below for the line of the main path rising up Easedale beyond the tarn and this will shortly join the ridge you are now on. There is no need to wait until you reach it; just continue along far enough to see that you are beyond the cirque of broken crags and then descend easy grassy slopes to meet the junction of the Easedale path with that leading up to Codale Tarn. Scramblers can enjoy the diversion of climbing the steep little crags of

Belles Knott on perfect rock, but those without such inclinations may now follow the main path down the slabs at the side of the Easedale Beck and then to the tarn itself. After that, the path is broad and well-used, down beside the foaming waters of the gill and back through the meadows to the footbridge and the tarmac once more.

Easedale Tarn from Blea Rigg

42.   *Whitbarrow Scar*

Best Map: OS 1:50,000 1¼" to 1 mile (2cm to
   1km) Landranger Sheet 97 (Kendal &
   Morecambe). (Not on 1:25,000 scale maps)

Distance: 5–6 miles/8–9.6km

Highest elevation reached: 706ft/215m

Height gained: 680ft/207m

Overall star rating: *

General level of exertion required: Low/medium

Time for the round: 2–2½ hours

Terrain: Fair paths through woods and along
   limestone scarps.

It was always the great cliff of White Scar which
caught my eye when I turned off the A591 to go
west to Eskdale and Wasdale, for as the road crosses
the estuary at the end of the Lyth Valley, it is clearly
visible for about two miles and the road passes just
below its foot. Then there were days when I retreated
from the Lakes because the weather was awful, only to
find that it was clearing as I neared Kendal – and then
I wished I had somewhere to go for a walk before

going home. White Scar is in fact the southern end of
a fine limestone escarpment about seven miles south-
west of Kendal and it looked a likely place. So I
explored. Forgive me if, for a few moments, I tell you
about my mistakes so that you don't repeat them.

On my first visit, I went below the great white cliff
of White Scar, found a way up to the top by its
left-hand end and then traversed along above the cliff
into the woods seeking a way down to the north-east.
Within two hundred feet of the car, I was almost
vertically above it and in thick forest and I had to
retrace my steps entirely.

Then I looked more carefully and worked out a
complete round that would start in the north-east at
the little hamlet of Row just beyond the Lyth Valley
Hotel, climb to the ridge, walk its length north to
south, descend White Scar and return along the
valley bottom using the paths and tracks clearly
marked on the map. This is perfectly feasible, so long
as you can arrange to be collected on your descent.
You'll have to climb a wall or two getting up to the
ridge, then you can walk its length successfully. But I
didn't have a driver and it is a complete disaster trying
to use the paths to get back to Row village, for even
when you find them, they're completely overgrown or
barred by barbed-wire. What should have taken an
hour at the most took me nearly two and a half, and

White Scar

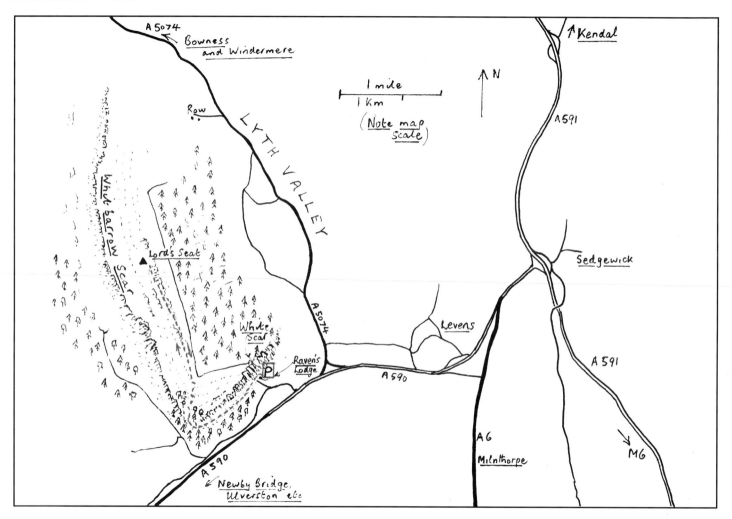

some ripped clothing. So, instead of a round, this time you'll have to go up and down the same way. But it really is worth it.

From the A6 or the A591, turn onto the A590 for Newby Bridge, Ulverston and the towns of west Cumbria. Just past the A5074 junction to Windermere, take the slip-road across the carriageway directly towards White Scar. Follow the signs for 'Raven's Lodge' and park just beyond the farm buildings (grid ref. 461852). A track climbs to the left below the huge cliff and runs out onto a great limestone pavement which I believe is called a 'bedding-plane' by geologists. It is surprisingly smooth and is exposed for about a quarter of a mile at the foot of the crags before it comes to an end. It was obviously used as a roadway for the former quarry operations. There is clearly no way of climbing to get above the scar until you have turned the corner, but the crags are becoming less steep as you approach it and they decline into a wooded shoulder, up which a pathway sneaks. You have little idea where you are for a while, but just stay on the path and you emerge onto the open heath above the woodland. Take notice of your position because you'll need to find it on the return. Now it's all space and open air; fine walking along the limestone edges. The awful massed conifers are fenced off just below the high land on the eastern side but on the heath there are only twisted junipers here and there and, in the area around Lord's Seat (the highest point) – where there is a large and solid cairn with a plaque commemorating Canon Hervey, Founder of

the Lake District Naturalists Trust – there are an enormous number of anthills, so be careful where you sit down.

As you retrace your steps, go just a little further to the edge of the White Scar cliffs and views over the estuary towards Morecambe Bay are revealed. All you have to do now is to remember how to get down.

On Whitbarrow Scar, near Lord's Seat

43. Holme Fell

Best Map: OS 1:25,000 S.W. Sheet (Wast Water and Coniston)

Distance: 4 miles/6.4km

Highest elevation reached: 1025ft/312m

Height gained: 700ft/213m

Overall star rating: * * *

General level of exertion required: Medium/low

Time for the round: 2½–3 hours

Terrain: Good bridle ways and paths except along the fell-top where sheep-tracks are helpful. (Competent scramblers could start at the other end of the fell and do one of the best low-level scrambles in the Lakes as well. *See* note at end.)

Scarcely noticed at the side of the winding and busy A593 road from Ambleside to Coniston, the traverse of Holme Fell is a delight. This walk starts at the north-eastern end of the fell, goes by tracks at a low level along its northern flank, visits the dramatic, disused quarries at Hodge Close, then climbs through lovely woodland onto the fell itself, before returning along its broad back. The fell-top is a most interesting and varied landscape and astonishingly little visited.

There are usually parking places on the minor road on the right immediately beyond Tongue Intake Plantation (grid ref. 329023). Now take the left-hand of the two metalled tracks leaving the parking area, go round a bend, up a short but steep hill and continue to High Oxen Fell Farm. Go between the buildings and follow the rough track (two gates, and downhill past a pond on the right) towards the first of the two giant disused slate quarries of Hodge Close. This is very impressive and it is possible to descend into it down a slope of slate-spoil leading to an archway through which the second quarry may be reached. The less adventurous will prefer to follow the track around between the cottages, turning left and so reaching the rim of this second even more impressive quarry which has a deep pool of dark water in its bottom. Take care when descending either way.

Continue around the rim of the second quarry and then, leaving the metalled track, go through a gate leading to a rough lane alongside a wall. Cross a stile beside a gate and continue along the lane through the trees until, forty paces before you reach yet another, turn off sharply left and uphill onto the fell. You have now left gates behind, until the very last. Ignore

Hodge Close Quarry

185

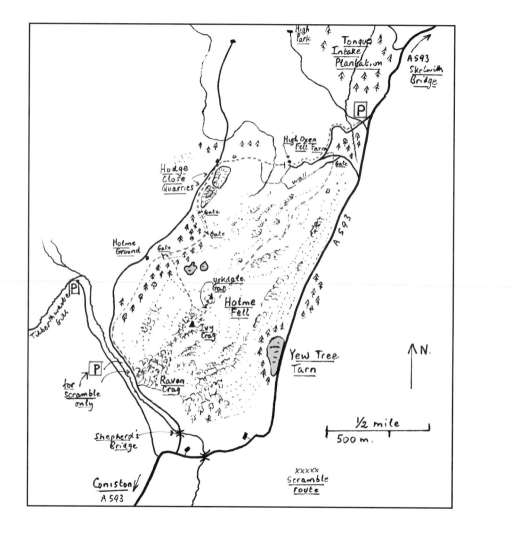

grassy paths which do not lead up towards a large cairn, clearly visible ahead and to the left. At the last minute, the path goes through the Uskdale Gap between the high ground on which the cairn stands and the actual highest point, which is the fine little Ivy Crag. Either scramble up or around to reach it, from where there will be extensive views of Coniston Water, Wetherlam and the distant Langdale Pikes.

There is now a path from Uskdale Gap down towards Yew Tree Tarn and the main road – but that would be a tame ending to a grand day.

Climb up to the large cairn and the broad top of the fell stretches to the north-east in a long, undulating, though at times not too obvious ridge, but which is going in exactly the direction you need to return anyway. Away you go, following sheep-tracks over and round little outcrops of rock amidst the bracken and heather and with fine views all the way, particularly towards the Fairfield–Helvellyn massif. As you gently descend towards the end of the ridge but still staying on the crest, a small tarn with numerous little grassy islets in it can be seen on the right, then some telegraph posts and a solid wall just ahead. Veer right along the line of the wall, and then for fifty paces along the wire fence which follows, to a gate which leads through this to a metalled road. Now turn left for fifty paces or so to a road junction, at which point you rejoin the outward route (and will see again the sign for High Oxen Fell Farm). All that remains is to walk back (north-east) the short distance along the road to the start.

Raven Crag Buttress, Holme Fell: *a superb alternative for competent scramblers.*

This is arguably the best low-level scramble in the Lakes and for competent and experienced scramblers (or for competent people accompanied by experienced scramblers or climbers) the ascent of the superb rock-rib on Raven Crag must not be missed. The start is at the Coniston end of the fell, grid ref. 311002, reached by taking the metalled track which leads over Shepherd's Bridge towards Holme Ground. There are a few parking places along the roadside near the foot of the crags. Then simply climb the stile which is just beside the first wall on the right (north) where it reaches the road and head up into the trees shrouding the foot of the crag.

Rock is reached almost immediately and the scramble begins by climbing a right-slanting groove just right of the very lowest rocks. Thereafter it is all on perfect rock, with marvellous situations and even an optional (and of course harder) hand-traverse at one point.

Reaching the top of the crag it is an easy walk to Ivy Crag, the highest point on Holme Fell. Now you should continue to walk as described earlier, along the fell-top and descending to the track near High Oxen Fell Farm, then on to Hodge Close Quarries. Leaving these and having reached the point (as described earlier) where you would have turned off the track to climb upwards onto the fell, simply continue along the track itself. This leads to the metalled one near Holme Ground and so back to the start.

The 'Lion and Lamb' on Helm Crag looking towards Dunmail Raise

PART FOUR

Walks in the South-East

44.   Elter Water, Colwith and Little Langdale

Best Map: OS 1:25,000 S.E. Sheet (Windermere and Kendal)

Distance: 5½ miles/8.8km

Highest elevation reached: 550ft/168m approx.

Height gained: 300ft/91m

Overall star rating: * * *

General level of exertion required: Fairly low

Time for the round: About 2½ hours

Terrain: Easy walking on good, though sometimes inevitably muddy, paths. No problems even when the mist is down to valley level.

This walk doesn't actually go up onto any fells, low or otherwise, but every fellwalker needs a few low-level walks for the off-day, the wet day, the family day. This is one of the best, with a splendid succession of little lakes, woods and waterfalls. Its description could however easily turn into a list of gates and stiles (the lower down you are, the more there are of them!) and you'd still get lost, so I will only mention the vital ones, because once you get going it is actually all very straightforward.

A footpath is signed to Skelwith Bridge from the car park in Elterwater village (on the other side of the road from the Britannia Inn). Grid ref. 327047. Follow this beside the Great Langdale Beck and then alongside the beautiful Elter Water, rambling through fine open parkland with mature trees until you reach a gate and enter a wood where the path goes along the road for a short way, and very close to the torrent of water at Skelwith Force, before passing between the buildings of Kirkstone (Slate) Galleries. The main A593 road to Coniston is reached here, so turn right (south) and cross the river by the road bridge and walk along the road for about a hundred paces towards Coniston before turning off right on the public footpath signed for Colwith Bridge. This path now climbs through a little wood (parallel with the main road), joins a farm track, continues beyond the farm (Park House) as a path again with views overlooking the Elter Water meadows you walked through a little while ago, past some incongruous permanently sited caravans and between the substantial buildings of Park Farm (where there is an intriguing 'alphabet stone' set in a wall on the left).

An arrow on another wall now points the way, keeping to the path and only crossing metalled drives, by-passing Low Park Farm, and leading across the slope of a field before descending through woods towards the River Brathay (flowing from Little Langdale Tarn) at Colwith Bridge and a stile onto the road

Elter Water and the Langdale Pikes

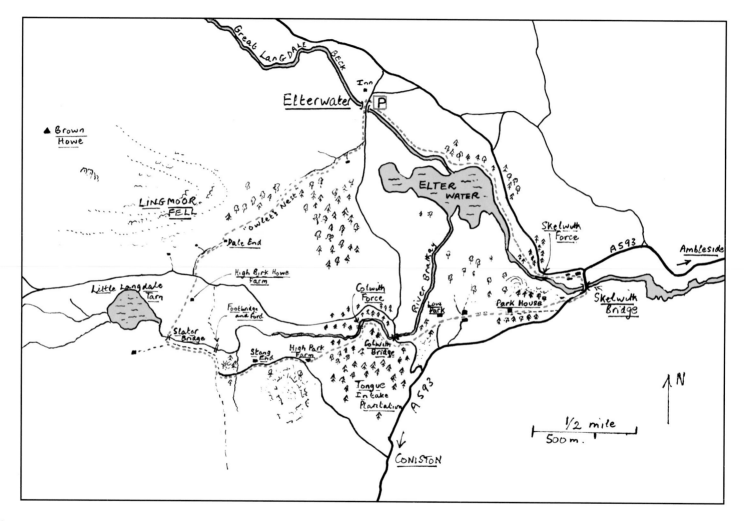

(Elterwater to Coniston). The fine waterfalls of Colwith Force are now close by upstream, so turn right along the road for fifty paces or so and climb another stile into the lovely woods (sign for Colwith Force). The better path meanders along above the river bank and soon the roar of the double cascade can first be heard and then seen, usually partly masked by foliage but a fine sight nonetheless. Attempts have obviously been made to harness the water-power as a little building at the foot of the torrent and to one side testifies.

Leaving the falls, the path continues through the woods on the left bank, climbing gently away from the stream and emerging by the buildings of High Park Farm. A bridleway passes between these and joins a metalled track just beyond them, giving, for the first time for some distance, the opportunity to see the line of the walk ahead as it crosses the valley bottom of Little Langdale and then contours right across the slopes of Lingmoor Fell. First, however, keep on the track as it winds round Stang End Farm and downhill over a cattle-grid, crosses a small beck, then curves round a tree-covered hillock to reveal a footbridge and a ford. If you cross here, you will miss one of the best bits of the walk so keep to the lane on the left bank which now has old quarry spoil on its left side. Beyond two gates, a stile in the wall on the right leads across to the gently pointed arch of the picturesque Slater Bridge. This spans the outflow from Little Langdale Tarn which can't be seen yet, though it soon comes into view, a lovely sheet of water backed

Slater Bridge in Little Langdale

by the Tilberthwaite Fells. The way now leads up the fields towards Lingmoor Fell via High Birk Howe Farm.

Just beyond the farm, the track meets the road which runs through Little Langdale. Turn left and then immediately right and you are on the track, not marked on the map but known, I believe, as the 'Owlet's Nest' track. After passing Dale Head Farm, this soon becomes a rough lane, often between stone walls and beneath the trees, with a few surprise views to the Helvellyn massif. Keep to the right when there is a choice of ways and you are soon back once more on the road outside Elterwater and at the end of a delightful ramble.

45. Loughrigg Fell

Best Map: OS 1:25,000 S.E. Sheet (Windermere and Kendal)

Distance: 4 miles/6.4km approx.

Highest elevation reached: 1099ft/335m

Height gained: 900ft/274m

Overall star rating: **/***

General level of exertion required: Medium

Time for the round: 2½ hours

Terrain: The early part of this walk uses sheep tracks when they can be found, but then joins substantial and well-used paths for the descent and return.

Loughrigg Fell is justly popular with fellwalkers of all ages for, although of no great height, it is quite a complicated little mountain and gives some outstanding views in good visibility. Even in poor visibility, the main paths are clearly marked but still Loughrigg Fell has some secret places.

Probably the most popular ascent – because it's the most obvious – is the short way from the top of the Red Bank road between Grasmere and Langdale and on any fine weekend a stream of pilgrims will be seen toiling up it. A much better walk circles Loughrigg Tarn on its western side and then climbs steep slopes to the north-east to the triple summits. The drawback can be parking problems. My proposed route is not so obvious as either of the ways mentioned above; it climbs more gently over much less trodden (though occasionally boggy) ground and allows a return along Loughrigg Terrace with its wonderful views over Grasmere and Rydal Water.

The start is about a mile out of Ambleside on the A591, just before you reach Rydal where a bridge crosses the River Rothay. Turn sharp left here and then immediately right over a cattle-grid to find the car park a hundred yards further on the left (grid ref. 365059).

Leaving the car park, slant up the field as if towards Ambleside and go through a gate in the wall. A narrow path rounds the fell and climbs up beside the fine little crag of Lanty Scar (in summer this can be through bracken as well), working up a broad gully to gain more height. The path soon becomes less obvious but it is not hard going and the gully leads to a rocky high point, at the end of a long, curving and very broad ridge, from where there are fine views over Rydal Water to Nab Scar and the Fairfield Group of

Loughrigg Fell seen from the boat-landing on Grasmere

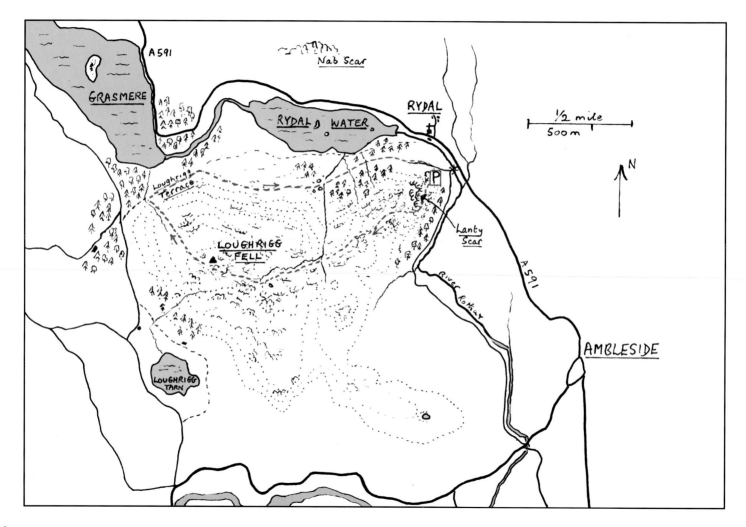

fells. Further along is another rocky point and beyond that again is a substantial cairn. These landmarks all give the direction to take, following sheep tracks through the bracken before descending a little to cross the main grassy bridleway that links Rydal with Langdale.

Beyond a short boggy section is a maze of sheep tracks but choose those that lead generally up a long slope, between many small crags and scattered juniper bushes, in the general direction of the highest ground ahead. A little tarn is reached, not much bigger than a large puddle, and then a well-worn and much-cairned path. This leads up a couple of short slopes and the trig-point on the summit of Loughrigg Fell is reached. Once revived and the views admired, it is straightforward now and downhill all the way, following the path to the north-west in the general direction of Grasmere. The landscape seen on the descent is really outstanding; I never tire of that wonderful outlook over Rydal and Grasmere surrounded by such fine fells.

At the end of the steep section, turn right and join the excellent level path that runs along the Loughrigg Terrace. This leads gently to the prospect over Rydal Water and then, keeping on the higher level when the choice is presented, skirt below first one and then the second great cave on the way back towards Rydal. Don't descend to Rydal Water's edge but keep on the path on the higher level. This soon reaches a tarmac lane and the car park is just a short way along it.

Grasmere from Loughrigg Fell

46. Grasmere and Rydal

Best Map: OS 1:25,000 S.W. Sheet (Windermere and Kendal)

Distance: 5½ miles/8.8km

Highest elevation reached: 500ft/152m

Height gained: 250ft/76m

Overall star rating: * * *

General level of exertion required: Low

Time for the round: About 2½ hours

Terrain: Some road walking but mostly on good paths and all at low level so that it is ideal even for a day when the mists are well down the fellsides.

The round of Grasmere and Rydal Water (or just Rydal Water) must be the Lake District's most popular low-level walk. It is rightly so and has been held in great affection by generations of Lake District visitors. It has great literary associations of course with the Wordsworths, De Quincey and Coleridge which enhance its appeal. But even if those names mean nothing to you, this is a beautiful walk. And, perhaps surprisingly, it is possible to make some little variations to it which will give a different perspective even to those walkers who may know it already.

When starting from Grasmere, the best car park is that in Stock Lane as you enter the village from Ambleside (grid ref. 339073). Now walk back and cross the main road, take the lane past Dove Cottage and the Wordsworth Museum and up the hill, past an overgrown little pond on the left, swing left and then right, still uphill. As soon as the road levels off, do turn off it and go up onto White Moss Common – astonishingly few people do and it is only a hundred yards' diversion – for one of the loveliest views in the Lake District, that over Rydal Water. On returning to the road, keep on the level and as the now unmetalled way curves round the bend, you can see where it continues into the woods below Nab Scar. The bend is where a beck tumbles down a gill here and the normal walk continues along the same level as before. However, for a variation, climb the stile and take the footpath up the left bank of the gill towards what looks like a little dam. When you arrive, you find there's a tunnel through it but also a narrow path going to the right over its top, above the trees outside the intake wall but just below the shattered crags of Nab Scar where juniper, ash, holly and hawthorn have all seized hold. This pathway continues at a higher level and out of sight of the ordinary path until

Rydal Water from White Moss

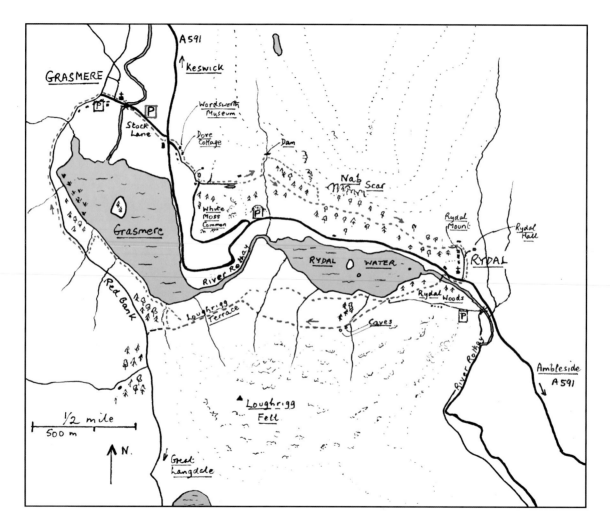

A591

↑ Keswick

GRASMERE

Wordsworth Museum

Stock Lane

Dove Cottage

Dam

Nab Scar

White Moss Common

Grasmere

Rydal Mount

Rydal Hall

RYDAL

River Rothay

RYDAL WATER

Red Bank

Loughrigg Terrace

Rydal Woods

Caves

River Rothay

Ambleside A591

½ mile
500 m

↑ N.

Loughrigg Fell

↓ Great Langdale

it rounds a corner and leads to a surprise on this steep hillside: a flat, grass sward about as big as a tennis-court – a marvellous place for a picnic.

Further progress at this level is blocked by a wall and steeper ground so you must descend and rejoin the main path, still delightful and now passing through woods and across sloping meadows, leading gently to the walled lane at Rydal, swinging downhill with the Mount on the right and the Hall on the left. Rydal Church is a little lower down and behind it the delightful Dora's Field, which – as well as an interesting brass plaque on a stone at its far end – also has some useful seats for contemplation of the sublime, or for just resting the legs.

Walk a few yards now to the main road, turn right and in another fifty take the footbridge over the Rothay, turn right and wander through the beautiful Rydal Woods. At the kissing-gate, you may continue beside the lake but it is more interesting to slant upwards a little to the wide gravel track which shortly climbs to pass the entrance to the lower of two great caves. Scrambling into this cave provides much fun for youngsters – and isn't as easy as it looks – but you can walk straight into the upper one.

Leaving the caves, follow the high-level path contouring the hillside below Loughrigg and well above Rydal Water, skirting above a wood of larch and birch to cross another shoulder for superb views of Grasmere. The path then leads round onto the level Loughrigg Terrace, from where more lovely landscape unfolds. Choose either a steep descent at the end of

the Terrace, or a slanting path before the end, towards the bridge over the Rothay at the outlet from Grasmere. Now take a path around the shore of the lake with views across the water to the little island and to the higher fells, all golden brown on their lower slopes and grey-green higher up. As the land becomes swampy, the path leads back to the Red Bank road. All that remains is the tarmac tramp down this road – the least interesting bit – but even now there are enchanting views over the wall and you soon reach the car again.

Grasmere seen from Red Bank

47.   Butter Crag and Allcock Tarn

Best Map: OS 1:25,000 S.E. Sheet (Windermere and Kendal)

Distance: 3 miles/4.8km

Highest elevation reached: 1150ft/351m

Height gained: 925ft/282m

Overall star rating: * * / * * *

General level of exertion required: Medium

Time for the round: 2 hours

Terrain: Easy walking on good paths though the descent may need care if wet, because wet grass at a steep angle can be lethal.

Allcock Tarn lies to the east of Grasmere on a rocky shelf, the northern end of which is Butter Crag, about halfway up the flank of the main ridge running from Nab Scar to Fairfield. It is a very pleasant ascent and usually below the cloud ceiling even on a wet day, giving views over the lovely vale of Grasmere. No wonder William Wordsworth enjoyed living here.

The most convenient starting-point is in Grasmere village at the Stock Lane car park (grid ref. 339073). Leaving this, turn left, walk back to the main A591 road and cross it to the secondary road signed for Dove Cottage and the Wordsworth Museum. Walk gently uphill a short way to a group of farm buildings, a reedy pond on the left and a crossroads, then turn left uphill (there's a sign 'Public footpath Allcock Tarn' on the roadside). In a hundred paces, the track leads off left again and quickly reaches a fork with a National Trust sign 'Brackenfell'. The left-hand track is closed by a gate in the wall, whereas the right-hand one leads upwards outside it. In fact, the right-hand way does lead, though more steeply and directly, via a kissing-gate, between walls and up alternately rocky and grassy paths, to Allcock Tarn, but it is not so pleasant as the left-hand way.

So pass through the gateway and follow the track which ascends through the trees, climbing in graceful curves up the fellside and with the occasional seat placed at a vantage-point. Pass a former circular fishpond and then, as the track rises above the woodland and becomes more of a path, skirt below and then rise up to the little rocky height of Grey Crag. This usually sports a flagpole as it is the highest point of the Grasmere Sports senior fell-race held in August each year. Some years ago, when I thought I

Greenhead Gill and Butter Crag seen from Grasmere

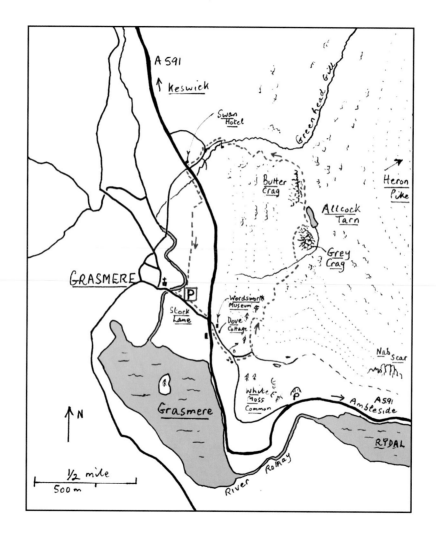

was fairly fit, I tried to see how far I could run up the course taken by the race. I did manage to actually run a little way beyond the first wall, slowed to a fast walk and then to a totter. I decided I wouldn't stand half a chance. I've been encouraged since, however, by noticing that during an actual race only a very few of the competitors can keep running further than that same wall.

Grey Crag is at the southern end of the shelf on which lies Allcock Tarn (not named on the OS map) so this is soon discovered by going on a little further and through the gateway in the wall. It can be a delightful sun-trap here; a most pleasant place to sit on the close-cropped grass and dangle your toes in the water.

To descend, follow the path leading alongside the tarn, over a stile at its northern end and then through a little rocky defile between Butter Crag on the left and the long uphill slope to Heron Pike on the right. Zigzags now lead downhill across the flank of Greenhead Gill and, keeping outside the wall, towards it. Once the shelter of the gill is reached, the trees shade the path which goes down it, a gate is reached, the path becomes a lane and, since there are now houses along the lane, it is metalled. Turn left at the junction and the main road is reached beside the Swan Hotel. Now go along the main road, but only for a hundred paces or so, before taking the (signed) public footpath on the right. This leads back via six gates or kissing-gates, easily and pleasantly across the meadows and so to Grasmere village again. The lads

(and lasses nowadays) who run the fell-race will all do the climb and be back in about twenty minutes – but they won't have had time to look at the view.

Storm clouds leaving Allcock Tarn

48. *Wansfell Pike and Troutbeck*

Best Map: OS 1:25,000 S.E. Sheet (Windermere and Kendal)

Distance: 6 miles/9.6km approx.

Highest elevation reached: 1581ft/482m

Height gained: 1400ft/427m

Overall star rating: */**

General level of exertion required: Fairly high on the way up, then easy

Time for the round: 3–3½ hours

Terrain: On good paths, but steep on the ascent. Most of the walk is at a low level and so enjoyable even in poor weather.

Wansfell Pike is actually the end of a long ridge running towards the Kirkstone Pass and it is easy to underestimate its ascent. But it does enable you to escape the crowds in Ambleside quickly, gives possibly the best view of the length of Windermere and, when combined with a return via Troutbeck, is a fine round.

The best car park is the main one on the left of the main road leaving Ambleside towards Keswick, just opposite the Charlotte Mason College (grid ref. 375046). Now head back towards the centre of the town to find the sign 'To the Waterfalls' which points between the Market Hall and Barclays Bank (itself next to the Salutation Hotel). A tarmac road now leads up the right bank of Stock Ghyll and after three hundred paces or so you should leave it to follow a track under the trees and very close to the rushing waters, for the beck comes down a series of cascades. There are plenty of seats and picnic spots and signs saying 'don't pick the flowers' or 'don't lean over the railings' and so on – for this a Beauty Spot and you'd better behave yourself.

Keep on the right bank towards a footbridge on the upper falls but bear right before reaching it and pass through the iron revolving gate which leads to a metalled road. A sign points the way up the road to Kirkstone Pass here and if you're ever inclined to walk up to Kirkstone on a quiet track, this is the way to go; if you try to walk up 'The Struggle', you'll be lucky to arrive alive. Walk up the road a little way and on the right there is a high ladder-stile and a sign to 'Troutbeck via Wansfell'. This is the way to go and the path climbs steadily but steeply, over more stiles and uphill through fields, with a final grind in low gear to the highest point. I must admit to a particular affection for the fine views now revealed, for I was just

The north-western slope up to Wansfell Pike from the Kirkstone Pass road

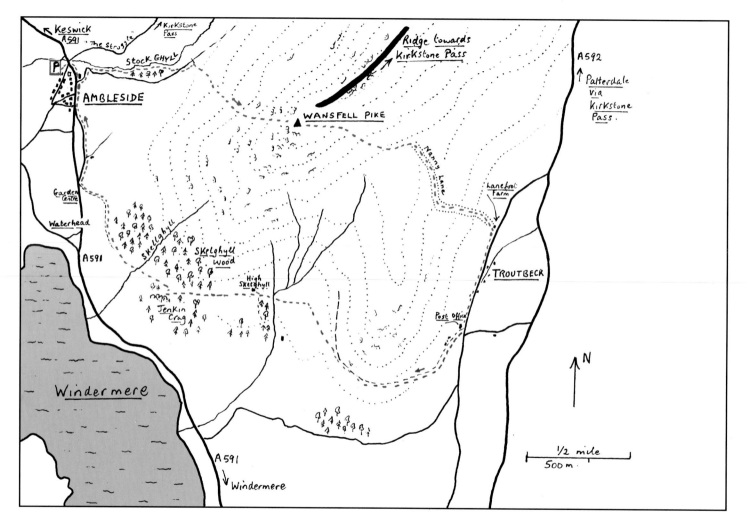

Keswick
A591
Kirkstone
Pass
The Struggle
Stock GHYLL
P
AMBLESIDE
Ridge towards
Kirkstone Pass
WANSFELL PIKE
A592
↑ Patterdale
via
Kirkstone
Pass.
Nanny Lane
Lanefoot
Farm
Garden
Centre
Waterhead
A591
Skelghyll
Skelghyll
Wood
High
Skelghyll
TROUTBECK
Jenkin
Crag
Post Office
N
Windermere
A591
↓ Windermere
½ mile
500 m.

fifteen when, from here, I first saw the wonderful Lakeland fells laid out before me, to which I have returned countless times. On a recent visit, even though the weather was fairly foul and I was being pelted with rain, I watched a rainbow arching between Loughrigg Fell and Snarker Pike, with the spire of Ambleside Church in the middle: a lovely, if transient, sight.

There is a stile over the summit ridge wall and a sign to Troutbeck via Nanny Lane. Follow cairns gently down the moor to the east to reach this walled bridleway which leads down, alternately grassy and slaty, very pleasantly to emerge on the road between the buildings of Lanefoot Farm. Turn right here and follow the road for a little under half a mile until you spot the 'Bridleway Ambleside' sign just beyond the village post office. This walled track climbs steadily until Windermere and then Wansfell Pike come into view again as it curves round the hillside. Now leave the track for the footpath on the left, signed to 'Ambleside via Skelghyll and Jenkin Crag', which leads across fields towards High Skelghyll Farm. When the path meets the metalled track leading to the farm, turn up it. It becomes a bridleway again beyond the farm and soon enters Skelghyll Wood. Halfway through the wood is the little rocky outcrop of Jenkin Crag which seems, on wet or fine days alike, to attract a steady stream of visitors. I think it's another Beauty Spot. There are views over the head of Windermere from here, but they are fairly well obscured by the trees.

Leaving the crag, the path begins to descend through the woods, crossing Skelghyll itself by a bridge and offering several alternative ways down. Keep to the highest path now as it soon reaches a tarmac lane which quickly leads to the old road just above Hayes Garden Centre. Turn right and you are soon back in Ambleside.

The Kirkstone Pass from Wansfell Pike

49. Silver How

Best Map: OS 1:25,000 S.E. Sheet (Windermere and Kendal)

Distance: 4 miles/6.4km approx.

Highest elevation reached: 1292ft/394m

Height gained: 1000ft/305m

Overall star rating: * *

General level of exertion required: Medium

Time for the round: 2½ hours

Terrain: A mixture of grassy, rocky and scree paths, almost all on the open fell.

Grasmere and Rydal Water are in the very heart of the National Park and Silver How is one of several minor fells whose ascent allows enchanting views over this delightful vale but is also a pleasure in itself.

Start in Grasmere village; the most convenient car park is that next to the new National Park Information Centre opposite St Oswald's Church (grid ref. 335074). There are many changes taking place in the centre of Grasmere but I hope it is safe to assume that the church will remain . . . From here, turn left, away from the village (on the road signed for Langdale and Coniston) which runs round the west side of the mere and then, avoiding the private drive across the meadow, go up the walled track opposite the boat-landings, clearly signed 'To Great Langdale'. This leads, via a kissing-gate, across a field with some fine larch and fir trees and also some splendid *roches moutonnées* (great rocks scoured smooth by moving ice and a reminder that it isn't so long ago that an Ice Cap covered the area) to another gate. Then pass up and across the hillside with the wall to your left which protects many fine trees from the depredations of the local sheep. The walls that keep out sheep don't keep out deer however and I have several times been for an early morning jog up the Red Bank road and seen them in the gardens of the houses along the way. When disturbed they leap and bound away into better cover and, from our experience, there are no such things as plants that deer will not eat.

There are good retrospective views from here across the vale, to Helm Crag, Seat Sandal and Fairfield and the fine gills that cut into their flanks. At the end of the rise the wall swings left and starts to descend and will lead eventually to Chapel Stile. Another path leads gently upwards across the fellside and, with a few kinks in it, will arrive at Harry Place Farm in

Silver How seen across Grasmere

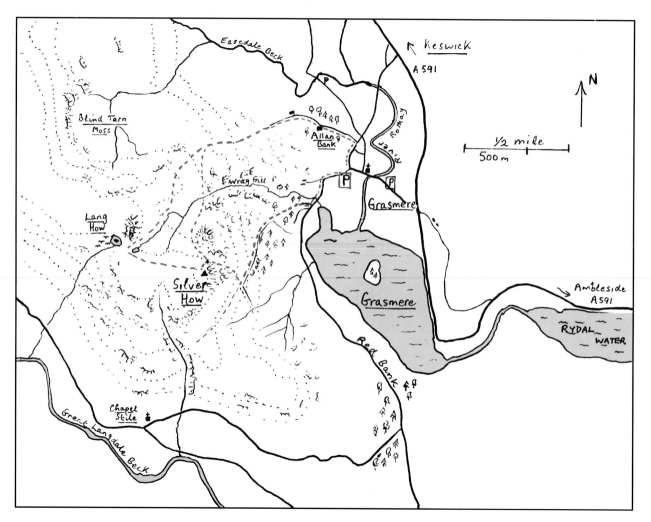

Easedale Beck

↑ Keswick
A591

N

Blind Tarn
Moss

Allan
Bank

½ mile
500 m

Ewray Gill

Lang
How

P

P

Grasmere

Silver
How

Grasmere

→ Ambleside
A591

Red Bank

RYDAL
WATER

Chapel
Stile

Great Langdale Beck

Langdale. Your way, however, should be still upwards, sharply right up the steep, grassy path which leads then up the little river of scree in a shallow gully. At the top, the view is over towards Easedale, and the summit of Silver How is just up to your left. The views are wide-ranging, particularly to the south-east; the shining waters of Grasmere, Rydal, Windermere, Coniston and Esthwaite Water can all be seen, as well as many lovely hills.

To descend, get onto the path heading down northwards towards Easedale. This skirts the edge of a depression or moss on Silver How's northern flank, in which rises Wray Beck, and just before the stream begins its plunge down the ravine of Wray Gill, the path crosses the stream into an area of juniper bushes.

If you fancy a further excursion before the descent, make your way along the fell-top towards the west (and the Langdale Pikes) where, about half a mile away, can be seen the rocky top of Lang How and, just out of sight below its crags, are two small tarns. The larger of these provides sanctuary during summer months for a screeching, squawking colony of black-headed gulls. If you get too close, however, you may well be warned away in a distinctly smelly manner. On leaving, follow the path north-west along the left-hand side of the moss, to reach the area of junipers at the top of Wray Gill.

The descent now continues steeply towards Easedale, over a stile, down a walled lane and so to a metalled one. This leads through open parkland beside Allan Bank, the beautifully situated house

which was home to William Wordsworth and his family for three years, then easily to Grasmere village again.

Turn right on reaching the Red Lion Hotel, and the car park is a few paces away.

Grasmere and Rydal seen from Silver How

50.   Helm Crag and the Easedale Ridge

Best Map: OS 1:25,000 S.E. Sheet (Windermere and Kendal), overlapping with N.W. Sheet (Ennerdale and Derwent)

Distance: 5½ miles/8.8km

Highest elevation reached: 1650ft/503m

Height gained: 1400ft/426m depending on how far you go along the ridge: valley level is at about 250ft/76m

Overall star rating: */* *

General level of exertion required: Medium

Time for the round: About 3 hours

Terrain: A steep ascent on a good path, then fair paths over peat and grass, which become stony on the last stages of the return.

The 'Lion and the Lamb' are distinctive rock features (not a pub!) on the summit of Helm Crag, the fell overlooking Grasmere village to the north, and provide an objective for a first-class walk. An alternative way to the one proposed – apart from just going straight up and down, of course – would be to descend to Greenburn Bottom to the north, but that would then involve a tramp back along tarmac. I prefer to return down Far Easedale.

Either park in Grasmere, or in the car park about a quarter of a mile up the Easedale road at grid ref. 334081 (there is no parking beyond here). Now walk up the road (straight on), past the turn-off to Easedale Tarn on the left, to the little hamlet at the end of the metalled section; Helm Crag will be directly in view ahead. Follow the signs for Helm Crag, through an iron gate and then a few paces up a walled lane, to reach a level green pathway. The old way used to go to the right here and then steeply up the shoulder of the fell but became very eroded, so there is now a new and better way, zigzagging much nearer to the main crag, past a very old quarry and then climbing steeply upwards for a little way using flat stones close-set in the bed of the path. This then passes directly above the top rocks of Jackdaw Crag, keeps curving left and climbs gradually to a shoulder, then goes right and up again on grass to another shoulder. A final steep bit up a rockier section leads to the ridge crest and a jutting little crag which overhangs the slopes above the Dunmail Roise road and must surely be 'The Lion'? But a little further along the crest another crag does exactly the same thing – and an enthusiastic scrambler with a good head for heights can climb to

Helm Crag seen from the descent from Allcock Tarn

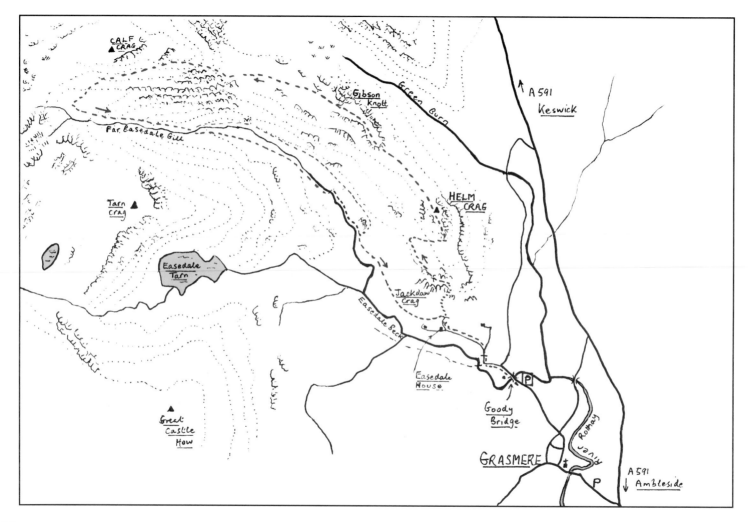

its summit. Both crags can look like the lion with the lamb at its feet, but it is the first that is seen best from Grasmere village.

The ridge stretches ahead but with a descent first to a saddle and then a climb up towards another rocky lump, Gibson Knott. You may descend from this saddle if you choose, for an infrequently-used grassy path leads down to the left towards a rock hump and then between two walls, to link up with the path along the valley floor of Easedale, but it's a pity to abandon this fine ridge so soon. The ridge-path skirts to the left of the main line of Gibson Knott, but it is more sporting to follow the ridge itself which, although broad, has quite a lot of scramble-worthy slabs.

Ending this section, further than it looks from Helm Crag, is another descent to a broad saddle furnished with several cairns – noticeable since cairns are unusual on this ridge. Some walkers do descend here to the north into Greenburn Bottom, but will have to face the eventual walk back along the tarmac that I mentioned earlier. The natural continuation however involves climbing gently upwards again up the blunt end of a steepening in the ridge towards its highest point (and that of the walk also) near Calf Crag. In fact, the path takes the easiest line and contours just south of the highest rocky bit, reaching a grassy hause at the head of Far Easedale. Here there is a short iron ladder-stile set firmly in a non-existent wall or fence: it is quite unmistakable and is a perfect guide even in the mist.

This is the point of return. An obvious path now leads in a south-easterly direction down the valley of Far Easedale, for about half a mile staying on the north bank of the beck, and then crossing over to the other side. It can be rather wet and boggy in places and although you can obviously stay on this path all the way down Far Easedale, you may find it worth-while not to cross over the stream but to stay on the

The 'Lion and Lamb' seen from the north side, looking towards Grasmere

217

Helm Crag and Easedale Ridge, looking down Far Easedale

north side a little longer. A narrow but very good sheep-track will be found shortly which contours down the valley at a higher level than the main path – and it is much drier. Just before the intake walls begin to close off the valley, this path reaches a large, ice-polished rock, at which point it is easy to go down the last bit of grassy slope to join the main path again which is now on the north side of the stream.

The final stretch goes along a most attractive part of the valley where rowans and holly bushes shade clear pools in the beck and there is many a tempting resting place in which to linger. Part of this last section is between the walls of an ancient lane which, in winter, can turn into a watercourse; it is therefore stony underfoot for a while but this soon leads to the foot of Jackdaw Crag where the outward route is rejoined. A turn to the right through the iron gate takes you back to the metalled road beside Easedale House and there remains just the stroll on the level road back to the car park.

ACKNOWLEDGEMENTS

Henry and Freddie

My debt to the Ordnance Survey and their wonderful maps will be self-evident. I have pored over them, searched my memories with their help and tramped over the fells with them in my pocket to remind me of details long forgotten. Although they are much more valley-based than my selection, I did find some good ideas in three little books from Polecat Press called *Walks to Remember* which I recommend.

My old friend Rob Rose accompanied me on several exploratory walks, my wife Lin and son Jonathan on others (and didn't complain much), but on the whole I have spent most of the time on the fells on my own with my two dogs, Henry and Freddie. Everybody else decided that waiting around while I took photographs is just too boring, so they left me to get on with it alone.

Index

Page numbers in **bold** refer to walks; those in *italics* to illustrations.

Aira Beck   103, 105
Aira Force   103, *105*, 105
Allcock Tarn   **203–5**, *205*
Ambleside   207, 209
Angle Tarn   91, *101*, 101
Angletarn Pikes   90, 91, **99–101**
Artle Crag   **79–81**

Bannerdale   91, 93, 101
Bannerdale Crags   *74*, **75–7**, *77*
Barrow   **41–3**, 123
Bassenthwaite Lake   45, 47, *47*
Beckside   121, 123
Beda Fell   **91–3**, *93*
Birkhouse Moor   *72*, 97
Birkness Castle   *71*
Black Combe   *120*, **121–3**, *123*
Black Crags   19, 25
Blake Rigg   *118*, *168*, **169–71**
Blea Rigg   *176*, **177–9**, 179
Blea Tarn   165, 169, 171
Blencathra   13, *15*, 19, 23, *40*, 75
Boardale   83, 91
Boardale Hause   83, 85, 91, 101
Border End   *140*, **141–3**

Borrowdale   21, 29, 31, 35, 39
Bowfell   19, 121, 141, *143*, 143, 145, 147, *171*
Bowscale Fell   *74*, **75–7**
Braithwaite   41, 43
Brothers Water   83, *110*, 111, *113*, 113, 115
Brund Fell   *32*, **33–5**
Buck Crag   90, 93
Buckbarrow   127, *128*, **129–31**
Butter Crag   *202*, **203–5**
Buttermere   57, 59, 61, 63, *64*, 65, **69–71**
Buttermere Fells   59

Carling Knott   *52*, **53–5**, *55*
Castle Crag   19, *28*, **29–31**, *31*
Catbells   *24*, **25–7**
Causey Pike   41, *43*
Cockley Beck   156
Cockley Beck Bridge   141, 157, 159
Cold Pike   156, **157–9**
Coledale   41, 43
Colwith   **191–3**
Coniston   161, 163
Coniston Fells   *139*
Coniston Water   161, 187, 213
Coppermines Valley   161, *163*
Crag Hill   41, *43*
Crinkle Crags   *143*, 147

Crummock Water   49, 51, 53, *55*, 56, 57, 59, 63, 65, 67, *70*

Dalegarth Falls   155
Deepdale   111, *113*, 113
Deer Bields Crag   *172*, 173
Derwent river   29, 31
Derwentwater   21, **25–7**, 29, 33
Dods   9
Dovedale   *110*, **111–13**
Dow Crag   141, 145, *147*, 147, 155
Duddon Estuary   *120*, 121, *123*, 123
Duddon river   137, 139
Duddon Valley   141, 151, 153
Dunmail Raise   *188*

Eagle Crag   39, 179
Easedale   **173–5**, 177, 179, 213, **215–18**
Easedale Beck   173, 179
Easedale Rigg   *218*
Easedale Tarn   173, 175, *176*, 177, *179*, 179
Elterwater   165, *190*, **191–3**
Esk Buttress   141, 145, *147*, 147, 155
Esk Pike   *143* 147
Esk river   145, 147, 155
Eskdale   125, 127, 133, 141, 143, *144*, 145, 149, 151, 153, 181
Eskdale Green station   *124*, 125, 127

Fairfield   97, 195, 211
Far Easedale   173, 175, 217
Fell Foot   171
Fell Foot Farm   *118*
Fleetwith Pike   61, **65–7**, *67*, 69

Gagale Crags   *51*
Gatescarth   **79–81**
Gatesgarth   63, 66
Gill Crag   *117*
Gill Grag Ridge   **111–13**
Glenderamackin river   75, 77
Glenridding   83, 87, 95
Gowbarrow Fell   **103–5**
Grange   31
Grange Fell   *32*, 33
Grasmere   173, 175, 177, 195, *197*, 197,
    199–201, *201*, **203–5**, 205, 211, *213*, 213,
    215
Grasmoor   *51*, 57
Grassguards   153
Grassguards Gill   *139*
Gray Crag   98, 99, 101, *114*, **115–17**, *117*
Great Castle How   *176*, **177–9**
Great Crag   36, **37–9**
Great Langdale   157, 165, 167, 169
Great Langdale Beck   165, 191
Green Crag   60, **61–3**, 70, **153–5**
Green Hill   *102*, 105
Greenburn Bottom   215, 217
Greendale   *128*, *135*
Greendale Tarn   129, 131
Greenhead Gill   *202*, 205

Greta river   21, 23
Grey Crag   **203–5**
Grisedale Pike   41, 43

Hallin Fell   87, *102*, *106*, **107–9**
Hallinhag Wood   87, 108
Hard Knott   **141–3**, 159
Hardknott Pass   141, 143, 145, 149, 151,
    153
Harrop Tarn   17, 19
Harter Fell   79, 81, 127, 136, 137, *148*,
    149–52, *151*, 153, *155*
Hartsop   99, 101, 111, 115
Haweswater   *78*, 79, *81*
Hayeswater   98, 101, 117
Hayeswater Gill   99
Haystacks   60, **61–3**, 63, 69, 70
Helm Crag   *2*, 175, 188, 211, *214*, **215–18**,
    218
Helvellyn   *2*, 13, *19*, 19, 87, 95, 101, *175*,
    175, 193
High Crag   *71*
High Doat   **29–31**
High Gait Crags   **145–7**
High Rigg   9, *12*, **13–15**
High Street   79, *85*, 93, 98, 101, 111, 115,
    117
Highnook Beck   53, 55
Hodge Close Quarry   *184*, 185, 187
Holme Fell   *160*, **185–7**
Holme Wood   *52*, **53–5**
Honister Pass   61, 65, 66, 70
Howtown   87, 91, 107

Ill Crags   141, 145, *147*

Jackdaw Crag   215, 218
Johnny Wood   29, 31
Jopplety How   **33–5**

Kailpot Crag   87, 108
Keldas   *72*
Keswick   21, *40*
Kettle Crag   *171*
King's How   35
Kirkstone Pass   83, 99, 115, 207, *209*

'L'al Ratty'   *124*
Langdale Pikes   *167*, 167, 169, 187, *190*, 213
Latter Barrow   *132*, **133–5**
Lattrigg   *20*, **21–3**
Lingmoor Fell   *164*, **165–7**, 193
'Lion and the Lamb'   188, 215, 217
Little Langdale   165, 169, 171, **191–3**
Little Langdale Tarn   *164*, 171, 191, 193
Long Crag   *147*, 163
Lord's Seat   *183*, 183
Loughrigg Fell   *194*, **195–7**, 209
Loughrigg Terrace   195, 197, 201
Loweswater   49, 53, 55

Mardale Green   79, 81
Martindale   108
Martindale Fells   91, *102*
Mellbreak   *48*, **49–51**, 57, 68
Muncaster Fell   **125–7**
Mungrisdale   75, 77

The Nab **91–3**, 93
Nab Crags *16*, **17–19**
Nab Scar 195, 199
Newlands 25, *27*, 59, 69

Outerside **41–3**, *43*, 43

Pasture Beck 115, *117*
Patterdale 83, 89, 107
Place Fell *82*, **83–5**, *85*, 87, 97, *109*
Pooley Bridge 91, 107

Rannerdale Knotts *10, 56*, **57–9**
Raven Crag 13, 75, 115, 187
Red Bank 195, 201
Red How *156*, **157–9**
Rest Dodd 90, 91
Rosthwaite 31, 35, 37, 39
Rothay river 195, 201
Roughcraggs Gill 157, 159
Rydal 197, 201, *213*
Rydal Water 195, *198*, **199–201**, 201, 211, 213

Sail 41, *43*
St John's in the Vale 13, 15
Sale Fell **45–7**

Sandwick 83, 87
Satura Crag 93, **99–101**
Scafell Pike 141, 145, 147
Scafells 19, 31, 66, 130, 131, 141, *151*, 151
Scalehill Bridge 49, 51
Scarth Gap 63, 70
Seatoller 29, 31
Sergeant Man 175, 179
Sheffield Pike *94*, **95–7**
Silver Howe *210*, **211–13**
Silver Point 86, 89
Skiddaw *12, 13, 19, 20, 21, 23*, 23, *44*, 47
Slater Bridge *193*, 193
Sourmilk Gill 69, 70, 173, 177
Spothow Gill 149, *152*, 153
Stanley Force **153–5**
Sticks Pass 95, 97

Tarn Crag *172*, **173–5**
Thirlmere *16*, 17, *19*, 19
Three Shire Stone 157, 159
Threshthwaite Mouth 115, *117*
Tilberthwaite Fells 163, 193
Troutbeck **207–9**
Troutdale 35, *35*

Ullscarf 17, 19

Ullswater *72*, 83, 85, 86, **87–9**, 89, 91, 95, 97, 99, *102*, 103, 105, 107, 117
Upper Eskdale 141, 143, 147

Wallowbarrow **137–9**
Wansfell Pike *206*, **207–9**
Warnscale Bottom 61, 63, 70
Wasdale 127, 129, 181
Wast Water 130, 135
Wastwater Screes *132, 133*, 135
Watendlath 19, 29, *32*, 33, 37, 39
Watendlath Beck *32*, 33
Watendlath Fells 36
Watendlath Tarn 37, 39
Wetherlam *159*, 159, 161, 171, 187
Whahouse Bridge 149, 151, 153, 155
Whin Rigg 127, *132*, **133–5**
Whitbarrow *183*
Whitbarrow Scar **181–3**
White Combe 121, 123
White Scar *180*, 181, 182
Windermere *164*, 209
Wrynose Pass 157, 159, 171

Yewbarrow 129, 131
Yewdale Fells **161–3**